The Frozen Coast

The Frozen Coast
Sea Kayaking the Antarctic Peninsula

Graham Charles, Mark Jones, Marcus Waters with Sarah Moodie

THE LYONS PRESS
Guilford, CT 06437
www.LyonsPress.com

The Lyons Press is an imprint of The Globe Pequot Press

First Lyons Press edition 2004

The Lyons Press is an imprint of The Globe Pequot Press.

10 9 8 7 6 5 4 3 2 1

Printed in China by Everbest Printing Co. Ltd.

© Photography: Graham Charles, Marcus Waters, Mark Jones
© Text: Graham Charles, Marcus Waters, Mark Jones with Sarah Moodie
Maps by Andrew Caldwell

ISBN 1-59228-442-6

Library of Congress Cataloging-in-Publication Data is available on file.

Contents

In memory of Sir Peter Blake
and with gratitude for his generous assistance

Forewords

I have had the good fortune to travel by small ice-strengthened vessels and even ocean liners down the Antarctic Peninsula on several occasions and it is a marvellous experience. But doing it in a kayak is quite a different kettle of fish.

Having once been instructors at the Sir Edmund Hillary Outdoor Pursuits Centre of New Zealand, and having spent a lot of their lives mountaineering and kayaking, Graham Charles, Mark Jones and Marcus Waters were very experienced in the out-of-doors and were very much at home in kayaks. They wanted a greater challenge so headed for the Antarctic Peninsula. Dodging great icebergs and battling against freezing temperatures, they weaved their way down great inlets and ultimately successfully concluded Antarctica's longest sea kayak voyage. They were brave and courageous men with a great sense of adventure – an example to all people who seek to extend themselves to the utmost.

Sir Edmund Hillary

In my opinion a sense of adventure is one of the most important aspects of the human character, for without it we are doomed as a species. I despair when I hear of school leaders cancelling outdoor excursions because of the concern over litigation, should something go wrong. Graham, Mark, Marcus and Adventure Philosophy are at the forefront of convincing us of the value of adventure. It seems crazy that we need convincing given that generations of young and old have revered the adventures of explorers and climbers who have gone where nobody has ventured before. Undeniably, there is an ongoing tension between those people who would eliminate risk and those, like me, who know that if we achieve that goal then the human species is certainly finished.

I was probably one of many who wanted to join Graham, Mark and Marcus on their southern paddle, but they were a tight knit group who knew each other well and quite sensibly stuck with their proven team dynamic. This dynamic and the trio's general adventuring expertise largely made up for their inexperience in polar sea kayaking. How many of us can look back on an audacious adventure and wonder how we were ever able to pull it off with so little experience – that great American climber and innovator, Yvon Chouinard, once said, 'Do the big things before you get too good'.

They were going into largely uncharted territory both geographically and technically, and their account of finding new equipment to deal with the extreme conditions rang a bell with me as I remembered times when existing equipment was simply not up to the venture I was planning, and I had to develop something new.

I salute Graham, Mark and Marcus for their sense of adventure and the sound planning that goes into their ventures. If future generations are to cope with the threats that are now becoming apparent they will need to be equipped with the attitudes and skills that are taught through adventuring. To achieve this, we need more people with courage and vision like Mark Jones, Graham Charles and Marcus Waters.

Graeme Dingle ONZM, MBE

Graeme Dingle is one of New Zealand's pre-eminent adventurers, with a lifetime of outstanding achievements in the greatest mountain ranges of the world, and an unparalleled circumnavigation of the Arctic. He is also a Founder and Executive Trustee of Project K, an initiative dedicated to youth development.

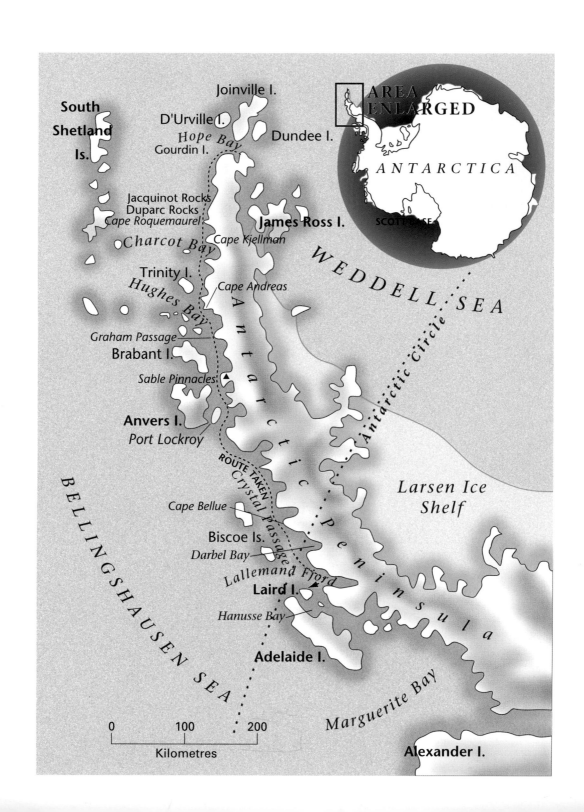

Joinville I.

South
Shetland
Is.

D'Urville I.

Hope Bay

Gourdin I.

Dundee I.

AREA
ENLARGED

ANTARCTICA

SCOTT ICE

Jacquinot Rocks
Duparc Rocks
Cape Roquemaurel

James Ross I.

Cape Kjellman

Charcot Bay

WEDDELL SEA

Trinity I.

Hughes Bay

Cape Andreas

Antarctic Circle

Graham Passage

Brabant I.

Sable Pinnacles

A n t a r c t i c

Anvers I.

Port Lockroy

ROUTE TAKEN
Crystal Passage

P e n i n s u l a

Larsen Ice
Shelf

Cape Bellue

Biscoe Is.

Darbel Bay

Lallemand Fjord

Laird I.

Hanusse Bay

Adelaide I.

BELLINGSHAUSEN SEA

Marguerite Bay

0   100   200

Kilometres

Alexander I.

Adventure Philosophy

Sarah Moodie

We believe in the spirit of adventure – being self-propelled, self-responsible, the need for an unstoppable attitude, the need for challenge. We believe that the world is a better place for those who are prepared to confront the improbable and defy the odds.

Antarctic Peninsula Sea Kayak Expedition mission statement

Where the swells of the Southern Ocean lash the implacable ice and rock of the Antarctic Peninsula, the roar is constant. Fortress-like ice cliffs guard the mountain ranges. Icebergs ride the swells like ships, obeying the hidden forces of currents and tides. Avalanches thunder into the sea.

In a rare bay breaching the sea walls float three men in sea kayaks, small splashes of colour in the vast wilderness of ocean and ice. It is late in the day. The men are bone weary, in need of a haven from the sea. One edges close to the rocks, awaiting his moment to land between the granite teeth of the cove. A big wave rears up behind him, sweeps him in a foamy grip towards the rocks. The besieged kayaker struggles with the sea. For these three specks of humanity on the edge of 14 million square kilometres of ice and rock, everything hangs in the balance.

One month earlier, New Zealanders Graham Charles, Mark Jones and Marcus Waters launched their sea kayaks into the cold water at the northern tip of the Antarctic Peninsula and turned south. Ahead lay an 850-kilometre journey along the icy no man's land between shore and ocean, where gales, waves and ice cliffs defend the Antarctic Peninsula against human intrusion. This long, exposed journey was to be the southernmost unsupported sea kayak trip ever undertaken.

The idea for the Antarctic Peninsula Sea Kayak Expedition was conceived in the mind of photographer, writer and adventurer Graham Charles. Already responsible for numerous firsts on whitewater, rock and mountain, Graham had taught, worked and played in the outdoors for most of his life. However,

An adventurous spirit lies at the heart of a healthy society.

it was not until the southern summer of 1997–98, that Graham first set foot in Antarctica as a field instructor at New Zealand's Scott Base.

One day that Antarctic summer, Graham stood where the cold black water of the Ross Sea laps at the ice. Two orca (or killer whales) porpoised fast towards him as orca do when they launch onto the ice to catch penguins. Ten metres and closing – Graham stood still, heart pounding, adrenaline racing in his veins. Several times before, he had turned and run at this point. This time, certain that he was being challenged to a game of 'chicken', he was determined to hold his ground. Five metres – close enough to see the piercing eyes, the battle scars on the flanks and the powerful muscles working to propel two tonnes of mammal through the water. And close enough to see the whales grin before they dived, at the last second, under the ice beneath his feet. Through the ice came a cacophony of squeals and clicks, while Graham went weak at the knees.

By the end of that summer Graham was in love with both the ice-bound continent of Antarctica and its wild coast. 'It was to do with being able to go places and find no sign of a single human, ever, in the whole of the history of the world,' Graham said. 'It was the sheer power of the place. The way the wind carves the rock, blasting it into ventifacts – solid rock sculpted and fluted by centuries of wind. Walking on Antarctica is like walking on a sleeping giant. It humbles you. In Antarctica there's no doubt about your own place in the world – and that place is minuscule.' His desire to return to Antarctica was profound.

As Graham pored over his maps and books, an idea formed: to paddle in sea kayaks from the northernmost tip of the Antarctic Peninsula to the start of the continental ice shelf. The Antarctic Peninsula jabs through the Antarctic Circle and reaches towards the southern tip of South America. The Peninsula is precipitous, its mountainous spine pushed up from the ocean floor after the break-up of the supercontinent Gondwanaland, some 150 million years ago. Although the continent of Antarctica lies perpetually under the frozen weight of 90 per cent of the world's fresh water, the western coast of the Peninsula sheds most of its load of sea ice during summer. It is hardly surprising, then, that exploration of the Antarctic continent began there.

The first human to set eyes on Antarctica did so at the Peninsula, in 1820. He was a young sealing captain. Sealers were responsible for much of the early exploration of the Peninsula during the 'fur rush' of the early 19th century – a monstrous massacre that brought fur seals in Antarctica to the edge of extinction. Both science and whales drew the next waves of humans to the Peninsula. In 1898–99 a Belgian scientific expedition under Adrien de Gerlache sailed down the Peninsula's west coast. As winter approached, their ship, the *Belgica*, became iced in, perhaps intentionally. De Gerlache's became the first expedition to winter over in Antarctica, a harrowing experience where one man died and another went insane. In the late 1890s and early 1900s, the waters and islands of the Antarctic Peninsula were busy with whaling boats engaged in a slaughter as heavy-handed and indiscriminate as the sealers'. Even then, French explorer and scientist Dr Jean-Baptiste Charcot, whose explorations and discoveries have been ranked as some of the most important in the history of Antarctica, noted concern about the fate of the whales if man continued hunting them in such a fashion. During 1903–05 and 1908–10, Charcot explored and charted the west coast of the Peninsula south of Anvers Island down to Marguerite Bay. He added greatly to Antarctic literature, with 28 volumes of reports, maps and charts.

With whale stocks depleted, the 'blubber rush' ended as sealing had done, but scientific interest ensured continued human presence and exploration in Antarctica. Today, scientific bases of various nationalities dot the coast of the Antarctic Peninsula. Although several countries active in the exploration of the continent made territorial claims to parts of it, all such claims were indefinitely deferred after the signing of the Antarctic Treaty in 1959. Antarctica is to be used only for peaceful purposes, with freedom of scientific investigation and co-operation. No one owns the continent, and anyone can go there if he or she can travel there safely. Every summer since the late 1980s, increasing numbers of shipborne tourists have visited, using the southern tip of South America as a take-off point for the relatively quick, but often rough, trip across the Drake Passage to the Peninsula.

Sea kayaking the waters of the Antarctic Peninsula, unsupported by yacht, ship or motor, was a daunting proposition. Had the idea been born in most other minds, it may have remained no more than a dream. Graham, however, had a gift rare in dreamers: the drive and ability to make his imaginings a reality. Whether achieving prominence in slalom kayaking and multi-sport racing, or making a name for himself in adventure photography, he pursued his goals with an intensity that 'leaves others gasping in his wake', as one friend put it. This competitive, achievement-oriented drive emerged in his teens, after his father's death in the mountains. The signature line of Graham's emails reads: 'We are what we repeatedly do. Excellence, then, is not an act but a habit'. Other favourite sayings include 'Whether you think you can or whether you think you can't, you are probably right' and 'Whatever you ardently desire, vividly imagine and enthusiastically act upon, will inevitably come to pass'.

Soon the Antarctic Peninsula sea kayaking idea was travelling through cyberspace to the computer screens of Marcus Waters and Mark Jones, at work in New Zealand. Graham's choice of people to share his dream was swift, but it was not arbitrary. Antarctic expeditions have a history of falling-outs and relationship breakdowns. As well as solid mountaineering and kayaking skills, Graham needed a team that would

The Adventure Philosophy Team. *Left to right:* Marcus Waters, Mark Jones and Graham Charles.

not splinter into acrimonious pieces under pressure. He needed people with complementary strengths and qualities, who were focused and prepared to make sacrifices for the sake of the expedition.

'Being simplistic, you could say I was the visionary, the leader, with Marcus being the details man, crossing the t's and dotting the i's,' Graham said. 'Compared to me, Marcus is a lot more precise and analytical – a linear thinker. I'm big picture, more vocal, more public and so I'd race around making plans and a mess, and Marcus would mop up and make sure it would work. Jonesy was our practical guru. I was dead keen to have him because I have no idea how to fix things, or skin an animal and eat bits of it.'

Marcus didn't need to think twice. 'Yeah, I'm into that,' was the response from the senior corporate human resources consultant of Christchurch. Born into a family of outdoor professionals and raised in the mountains, rivers and sounds of Marlborough, Marcus was a skilled and qualified outdoorsman, and

There are no ordinary days in Antarctica – as good as it gets in the Lemaire Channel.

a dedicated flatwater kayak racer. He had a long history with Graham: years of friendship, shared expeditions and later teaching outdoor skills at the Sir Edmund Hillary Outdoor Pursuits Centre of New Zealand (OPC) in the central North Island.

'At school there were three of us – Graham, Willy McQueen and me – who did trips together,' Marcus said. 'Willy was the cautious one. I was the most out there, and Graham was in between, often making the final call between me or Willy. Graham is not a reckless person and he usually operates well within his skill level. I've become more like that these days. When I was younger I thought only in terms of meeting the challenge, no matter what. If there was something to climb, that was the goal, obstacles regardless, end of story. But after a few prangs over the years I'm more cautious. Now I'm much more rational about what I do and don't do, whether I have what it takes technically to do something or not.'

Absorbed with the mental and physical endurance of long-distance flatwater kayaking, Marcus found the thought of a long, hard sea kayak expedition appealing. 'Antarctica isn't a shrine to me, so it wasn't so much a mystical pilgrimage as the physical adventure, the endurance aspect of getting from A to B, which motivated me.'

Mark Jones, known to all as 'Jonesy', was more measured in his response to his friend's enthusiastic proposition to do a 'mission on the ice'. Easy-going, quietly spoken, cool under pressure, Jonesy was an experienced outdoor educator with the technical skills to operate at a high level in a wide variety of terrain from whitewater to rock, cave to mountain. It was as an outdoor instructor at the Sir Edmund Hillary OPC that he met Graham and Marcus.

In addition to his other talents, Jonesy possessed a set of skills neither Marcus nor Graham had. Born to an inventive hunter father and an adventurous aerobatic pilot mother and raised on a farm where improvisation was necessary to keep the equipment running, he could hunt, fix anything and was self-reliant in the wilderness. 'At OPC he would go hunting in the morning before breakfast,' Marcus recalled with some disgust. 'He'd come back with these deer carcasses which he'd hang right outside our window to clean, while we were eating breakfast.'

Jonesy considered Graham's idea critically. 'It didn't sound totally attractive to me. I had never sat in a kayak for more than two or three hours without an old back injury giving me grief, and most of what I knew of Antarctica was written about men with frozen beards seeing how dead they could get. But I did love an adventure. I emailed back and said, "Yeah, but not if it's been done before." '

The fact that the Antarctic Peninsula expedition would be an adventuring first sealed it for Jonesy, but his problematic back meant he now faced a major challenge to cope with the physical side. 'Jonesy was a gamble in that respect,' Graham said. 'But he's always been a dark horse, full of surprises. I told him to get out and train hard, paddle and paddle and see if he could stand up to it.'

In today's world, our level of competence and decision-making skills determine whether we earn praise or censure, a good living or an average one. Mostly we can walk away from our mistakes with little more than the knowledge of failure. But for those who venture out of the comfortable, civilised world, survival itself can rest upon nothing but individual judgement and skill. So why do it? For the same reason that adventurers through the ages have stepped beyond the realms of the known. For the reward of being the only human for hundreds of miles. For the sight of nature at its most wild and spectacular. For the glee that springs from challenging nature and surviving. For the need, in a world overrun and tamed by humankind, to be no more than a speck in the wilderness. For the belief that the world is a better place because of those who confront the improbable and defy the odds.

Without having looked at a detailed map of the coastline, and without more than a general understanding of the environment, the three friends committed themselves to the adventure: Graham the leader, the dreamer, the motivator, the man in love with Antarctica; Marcus the planner, the details man, who revelled in physical challenge; Jonesy the practical guru, the quiet guy whose feeling for wilderness and adventure verged on poetic. Different characters with different strengths and motivations, they shared one fundamental principle: a belief in adventure. This belief crystallised with the creation of Adventure Philosophy, an organisation that would act both as a vehicle for the Antarctic Peninsula Sea Kayak Expedition and future expeditions, and as a flag bearer for the concept of adventure in the 21st century.

'Adventure Philosophy believes in an adventurous spirit – the determination to pursue a dream or vision, the tenacity to overcome barriers, a willingness to take calculated risks, and a respect and affinity for the earth,' reads the script at the top of the Adventure Philosophy website (adventurephilosophy.com). 'Adventure Philosophy believes an adventurous spirit lies in the heart of people that make up a healthy society. We share a philosophy of small self-contained teams embarking on adventures which leave no trace of their passing. Adventure Philosophy aspires to set a valuable precedent to the increasing numbers of people visiting our valuable remote wilderness areas.'

In an interview with the *New Zealand Listener*, Graham explained the reasons underpinning the philosophy. 'New Zealand was famous in the past for its mountaineers and adventurers… but adventure is being redefined as a bungy jump and a jet boat ride in Queenstown. We don't want to lose the roots and foundation of the adventure philosophy, that attitude of old where adventurers looked at maps and said "What if?"'

Antarctic sunsets are long and exquisite – Lippman Island Group.

Talking to the *New Zealand Herald*, Jonesy turned to the words of 18th century poet, dramatist and scientist Johann Wolfgang von Goethe to emphasise the necessity for adventure. '"Man can withstand anything except a succession of ordinary days." Goethe said that in the 1700s. It is as true today as it was then,' Jonesy said. 'We live in the most amazing country in the world, yet young people would rather be in the virtual world than the real one. I want to get them out of the video parlours and into life.' He summed up the expedition's philosophical goal: 'I hope our quest will inspire others to chase their dreams whatever they might be. None of us dreams alone. One dreamer breathes life into the next.'

By early 1998, the team members were chosen and burning to confront the challenge they had set themselves. In every way it was to prove a far greater task than they could imagine.

The dream had a shape, but it was an outline only. As the team began to prepare for the expedition, a fuller picture emerged. Slowly, the seriousness and complexity of the undertaking dawned. With hindsight following the expedition, Jonesy later wrote:

> *Had we reconnoitred the Peninsula with a mind to paddle it we would never have made the attempt. The coastline is simply too exposed, landings too few and far between, and the weather when it decides to play rough, just too formidable. But we had a dream to adventure in the Antarctic and we publicly declared our bid before we laid our hands on any maps of the Peninsula. We were not constrained by preconceptions of what was possible and what was not.... Ignorance can be a powerful ally sometimes.*

Kayaking in Antarctic waters is not new. In his report on a year-long Joint Services exploration of Brabant Island in 1983, Commander Chris Furse laid claim to the 'first real canoeing in Antarctica' when members of his expedition circumnavigated the island in three kayaks supported by motorised inflatable boats. The 160-kilometre trip was completed in three weeks. Eleven years later, in 1994, Australian sea kayakers Wade Fairley and Angus Finney paddled around the Argentine Islands, Port Lockroy and Paradise Bay. In addition, various expeditions, tours and charters to the Antarctic Peninsula have used kayaks for short day excursions in good conditions.

No one, however, had attempted an Antarctic kayak journey of anywhere near the distance, duration or exposure planned by Graham, Jonesy and Marcus. As the three men began to research their adventure, it became apparent that the expedition hung upon four crucial factors: landing places, sea ice, wind and money.

The sea surrounding Antarctica is full of ice of all sizes from huge tabular icebergs to a mass of small chunks, known as brash ice, which is blown about by wind. When it is thick, brash ice can block channels and fill bays, forming a barrier that can halt progress altogether, prevent landings and trap the expedition. During some seasons, for example, the Gerlache Strait can become an impenetrable jostling mass of ice. 'We would be screwed if that happened – and the Gerlache is halfway through the trip,' Marcus said.

The questions of whether and where the kayaks would be able to land on the inhospitable coast were just as critical. Yachts and ships provide mobile, floating havens for their crew and passengers, but kayakers need to land daily to eat and sleep. Weather that might see sailors reef their sails would send a kayaker racing for the shelter of land. Any stretch of coastline with no known landing places presents a risk.

Maps show that the first 200 kilometres of the coast south of Hope Bay are isolated and exposed. With almost no shelter from offshore islands, the swells and storms of the Drake Passage smash into the cliffs. The *Oceanites Site Guide to the Antarctic Peninsula* says the northwest coast offers 'few and widely separated possibilities for landing or Zodiac cruising'. In contrast, the middle section of the journey would offer a comparative sanctuary, with coves for landing and numerous offshore islands providing shelter from ocean swells. Scientific bases and stations are scattered on this section of coast and its islands, and it is a popular area for tour and charter boats. But few modern-day charter expeditions venture beyond the southernmost station, Vernadsky, on the Argentine Islands. Maps south of Vernadsky Station show the coast carved by deep bays and fiords with few, if any, landings apparent for 200 kilometres. The mountain ranges rise sheer from the sea and giant glaciers plunge into the ocean. Islands and the odd cape offered the only possibility of landing. Of the entire coastline, there was least information about this dramatic southern section.

For first-hand advice, Graham approached Antarctic veteran and wilderness photographer Colin Monteath, whose stunning images of the Peninsula had added fuel to Graham's desire to go there. In his extensive photo library in Christchurch, Monteath pulled out maps of the coast and explained the geography. Drawing upon 25 seasons of experience in the area, Monteath tried to drive home the gravity and complexity of the undertaking. 'I was pretty sure there were no landings in certain sections,' he said. 'You wouldn't want to get caught in a storm in those places.' Maybe, however, Monteath's passionate enthusiasm for Antarctica tempered his words of caution because Graham came away feeling heartened about the prospect. According to Marcus, 'It was probably the strength of Colin Monteath's opinion that made us think that our plan wasn't completely insane.'

Jonesy, assigned the task of organising the maps, hunted through books, articles, guides and research papers for information which he marked on the maps. He noted popular landing places, refuge huts and stations. He also highlighted penguin colonies, figuring that if penguins could land, a sea kayak stood a good chance. Yet most of the information was vague. The *Antarctic Pilot*, designed for yachties and skippers with detailed information about reefs and shoals, and other navigating hazards, simply described vast sections of coast as 30-metre ice cliffs for hundreds of kilometres. 'The BAS SP403 states that the entire coastline of this map is ice and rock cliffs – big enough to be marked on a 1:250,000 map,' Jonesy emailed to Marcus and Graham at one point. 'All this was incredibly discouraging,' Jonesy said, 'but it never seemed to faze Graham or Marcus. They seemed to have decided we were going, no matter what.'

If geography was one issue, weather was another. Extremely cold easterly winds whipping off the continent deflect northwards when they hit the mountains of the Antarctic Peninsula. The east coast is frigid and ice-bound. In contrast, conditions on the west coast are more temperate. Summer sees 24-hour daylight, temperatures between −6 and +6° Celsius and winds travelling up and down the coast in roughly equal quantity. Tides would not be big, and the circumpolar current was basically working in their favour, although close to land this was countered by an eddy effect.

The element the team feared most was a singular wind – the katabatic. Born inland in the elevated, cold interior, katabatic winds pour down towards the coast at high speed, flowing out of fiords and bays like rivers of air. Katabatics can reach gale force in less than half an hour, with little warning. A sea kayak caught in a katabatic during an exposed bay crossing could quickly be blown out to sea. The only information the team could glean about katabatics was anecdotal: watch out for caps of cloud over the mountain on clear days. 'We were the new guys and we had to learn quickly,' Graham said. 'We couldn't sit on the beach until we knew the finer details about how a katabatic comes along. We didn't have time to be conservative. I hoped that mostly we would be able to run and hide.'

In spite of their efforts to fill the gaps in knowledge, it was obvious that many of their questions could be answered only in Antarctica. 'Ignorance may have helped us overcome any qualms more experienced people would have had,' Jonesy said. 'We also had incredible belief in ourselves, and I totally drew on Graham's faith that we could do it.'

'I back myself,' Graham said. 'Maybe 15 years ago that would be bravado, but now I have a lot more tangible strength of judgement, and also an inner sense of the environment, a subtle intuitive awareness of knowing when I'm safe running it out.'

If it did not seriously occur to any of the team that the expedition could end badly, it lurked in the minds of others. 'Marcus's dad has spent quite a bit of time down on the ice,' said Marcus's partner,

The biggest threat on the journey were katabatic winds, which can turn the sea from mirror calm to a maelstrom in less than half an hour.

Wind, water and sun combine to create extraordinary icebergs.

outdoor educator Erin Boardman. 'I remember him saying there were some really strong winds, and questioning if they could do it. That's when I started to think that it sounded a bit serious.'

'I just wanted Jonesy to come back,' said Jonesy's wife Sally Rowe, an experienced outdoor professional in her own right. 'I knew that if something happened to one of the boys, the other two would risk their lives to save him. And while I had confidence in them, they didn't have the answers to lots of details about the weather and the coast and that worried me. But for them, that was a big part of the adventure: the unknown.'

Before the team could confront whatever Antarctica held in store, there was a more immediate hurdle to overcome. Not only is Antarctica one of the most isolated and inhospitable places in the world, it is also one of the most expensive to visit. Most expeditions to the Antarctic Peninsula depart from the southern tip of South America, crossing the Drake Passage in a matter of days. The cost of chartering a boat to drop the team at Hope Bay and pick them up further south was around $NZ60,000. Add airfares to Argentina, boats and equipment, and the total cost checked in at around $NZ130,000. If the expedition was to get off the ground, the team needed sponsorship, and not only gear, but some serious cash.

Full of hope and great expectations, Graham set about knocking on the doors of outdoor equipment manufacturers, while Marcus wrote letters to businesses and companies asking for sponsorship. Soon, the results began to roll in: 'Dear Marcus, I regret I cannot help you at this time'; 'Dear Mr Waters, We have considered your proposal but decided to decline'; 'Dear Marcus, We are unable to take on any new sponsorship initiatives at this time'; 'Dear Marcus, As much as I would like to be able to support your upcoming journey, I require more justification than a respect for the challenge you have set yourselves'. Spirits soared when Natural History New Zealand proposed to make a movie of the expedition, paying for the trip over there. A month later, though, hopes crashed when the project was canned.

By mid-1999, one and a half years after the expedition had been conceived, some progress had been made. Sea kayak company Paddling Perfection was lined up to design and manufacture sea kayaks. MSR in the United States had come on board with stoves. A deal had been made to publish a book. Graham drew upon his established relationship with reputable New Zealand outdoor gear company Macpac, to obtain a tent and top-range expedition clothing, including specifically designed polar kayaking suits and life jackets. Macpac spokesperson Kate Ward said the company had seen an opportunity to put its gear on one of New Zealand's best kayakers in an extreme environment. 'We look for people who are role models, icons, doing inspiring things, committed to the outdoors. Graham is talented in his field, has the respect of people in the outdoors, and the nature of his personality makes him exciting for the media. He has the potential to be the next Sir Peter Blake. Sir Peter was that way too: he just captivated people.'

Critically, there was still no money and therefore no way of getting the expedition to Antarctica. The true magnitude of the task facing the team was becoming apparent. 'When we first started, we thought the expedition was such a cool thing that everyone would bend over backwards to be involved and help us,' Marcus said. 'But it became abundantly obvious that this was not the case. We got a resounding "not interested", and we realised it would require more effort than we originally anticipated.'

The decision was made to put the trip back a year, to the summer of 2000–01, giving more time for fund-raising and in-depth preparation. 'We had to be smarter, target the right people,' Marcus said. 'And although initially we'd agreed that Graham would get the gear together, I'd go for money and Jonesy would do practical stuff like sort out the maps, it became obvious that funding was the biggest job and we had to share it to cover enough ground.'

By the start of 2000, the team had planted so many seeds through word of mouth and letter, that, in the midst of a steady stream of rejections, some sprouted. The first tangible financial gain came when

Jonesy won a $3,000 scholarship from New Zealand insurance company AMP. This gave the boys a surge of energy. Not only had the team publicly announced their plans, but someone had actually committed their money to it. It was a psychological boost, but there was a long way to go. In the last week of July 2000, two major hopes for a significant sum of money remained: a sponsorship deal with Compaq, which seemed extremely promising, plus the fact that Jonesy was into the second round of AMP scholarships, this time for $20,000. 'I talked to Jonesy that week,' Marcus said. 'I said *one* of them, at least, has to come off. I just didn't believe it was possible that neither would. I was utterly depressed the next week.'

Pressure was high and mounting, exacerbated by the fact that several sponsors had already committed considerable resources and time to the trip. Awaiting trial was Macpac's polar sea kayaking clothing, plus three polar sea kayaks that had emerged from the Auckland-based workshop of Ron Augustin and his company Paddling Perfection. Augustin devoted around $NZ30,000 to designing and testing kayaks that could endure cold, ice bashing and rocky surf landings, and were stable enough for tricky water-to-ice exits, deep enough to carry a lot of gear and yet sufficiently fast for long-distance paddling. It was a challenge, but Augustin, the 'mad scientist' of New Zealand kayak manufacturers, called upon 20 years of kayak designing experience and came forth with the Polar Bear sea kayak. 'There could be no turning back for the boys once they were down there, so the boats had to be completely bulletproof,' Augustin said. He wasn't exaggerating: five layers of kevlar can stop a 0.303 calibre bullet in a bulletproof vest. Three layers of kevlar reinforced the Polar Bear's bow against ice and surf landings. All the components were tested in the deep freeze to see whether they could withstand polar temperatures.

By early September, despite a considerable campaign, Jonesy's $3,000 AMP scholarship remained the only significant cash raised. Then, a miracle. Some months beforehand, Jonesy had approached New Zealand yachtsman Sir Peter Blake to see if there could be some tie-up between their trip and Sir Peter's upcoming expedition to Antarctica on his yacht *Seamaster*. The noncommittal response from the icon Kiwi adventurer did not leave Jonesy with high expectations.

Unknown to the team, Sir Peter made some enquiries of his own. 'Three Kiwi kayakers wanting to do what no one had done before,' Sir Peter wrote later. 'Who could refuse their request for a lift? I made sure they were properly qualified before becoming involved, however. We knew it was a huge undertaking, but they had prepared well, which gave us every confidence that we were highly likely to see them alive at the end of their venture.'

Sir Peter's offer was three free berths on the *Seamaster* from Ushuaia to the tip of the Antarctic Peninsula. The passage was a one-way ticket, and their return lay unresolved for many weeks. Salvation came in

Long days, no landings and constant uncertainty are the staple diet of Antarctic kayaking.

the form of a film deal when Queenstown-based producer James Heyward won approval from American Adventure Productions to shoot a documentary film of the trip. The team would pay for a third of the boat and shoot most of the expedition footage, in exchange for a ride home. A 14-metre yacht called *Tooluka* would meet them for the final few days of their journey.

At last the trip, which had been flying on the wings of faith, was on solid ground. 'When Peter Blake called us, I knew for the first time that the expedition would definitely go ahead,' Marcus said. 'And everything began to snowball from that point.'

In the early days of preparation, the team had made a series of educated guesses and drawn up a massive list of gear. Jonesy and Marcus put together a menu based on a diet analysis programme from the Auckland University of Technology and information from the Iridium Ice Trek website. (Ice Trek was the

1998 journey to the South Pole by Eric Phillips, Peter Hillary and John Muir.) In the final months of 2000, as more equipment sponsors offered support, more ticks began to appear on the vast list of food and gear requirements. (For details see equipment chapter.) For Neville Jones, whose company Mapworld donated GPS (global positioning system) equipment, it was his first serious sponsorship. 'It grabbed me,' he said. 'I thought it was a fabulous adventure, and even though we are a relatively small business, we were keen to support it.' And at last, cash sponsorship – including a $US8,000 grant from Polartec, which was impressed by the complexity and seriousness of the expedition – began to swell the Adventure Philosophy bank account.

Seeking an Antarctic-like environment for field trials, the team headed for the stormy, mountainous coast of Fiordland, and the freezing, terminal lake of the Tasman Glacier at Aoraki/Mount Cook, complete with icebergs. This would prove to be invaluable. At Milford Sound the team packed their boats heavy with cans, potatoes and water to see how they would handle fully laden.

They set off south as the Fiordland coast was being hammered by strong southwesterly winds in a grim spring weather cycle. After two days of fighting the wind, their plans to paddle the open coast from Milford to Doubtful Sound seemed overly optimistic. A weather map from a passing fishing boat showed two menacing cold fronts lying across the Tasman Sea like raised eyebrows, and behind these a deep depression was tracking their way. They turned back north, plugging into a strong nor'westerly head wind. It took them five hours to gain a mere 15 kilometres, and each hour they feared the rising wind would have the last say.

The weather may have thwarted their plan to paddle to Doubtful Sound, but it provided a chance to test their paddle fitness and endurance. Graham and Marcus had been steadily building on an already considerable fitness base; Marcus putting in daily flatwater sessions lasting between one and four hours and Graham combining frequent whitewater paddling with weights and two flatwater sessions a week. Both men had a proven history in long-distance kayaking and multi-sport racing, but the third team member was an untested quantity. For Jonesy, whose kayak training on the water and in the weights room had been plagued by pain from old injuries, the Fiordland trip was a revelation. 'Up to that point, I almost did not believe the Antarctic trip would happen for me,' Jonesy said, 'because I could not shake my back problems. I left Auckland struggling to paddle for more than three or four hours without pain, feeling pessimistic, expecting to be coming home after one day. But down there, I felt good and paddled really well. That was the first time I really believed I would go.'

At Aoraki/Mount Cook, where the Tasman Glacier melts into an ice-filled lake, the three found a near-polar environment to test gear and skills which, if found wanting, could be fatal in Antarctica. They practised rescues, bailed out of their boats into the icy water, tested their new Macpac drysuits. They discovered just how quickly hands become useless in freezing water, and trialled a prototype pogie (glove) designed from closed-cell foam. From their boats, they donned crampons and climbed out onto icebergs, in case of forced landings.

Importantly, they also had a chance to test team dynamics and discuss the human aspect of the expedition. The day they headed south, the *New Zealand Herald* ran a story about the ill feeling festering in the wake of the Iridium Ice Trek Expedition. It was a timely reminder. Intense experiences concentrate emotion and can test the strongest friendships. Characteristics that seem agreeable under everyday circumstances can become unendurable during the close, pressured conditions of an adventure. Conscientious attention to detail can seem unbearably pedantic. An easy-going approach can seem intolerably thoughtless and messy. A direct opinion can seem insufferably overbearing and offensive.

Before they left Jonesy wrote:

> In the Antarctic we know we will get tired. We will get frustrated. We will see sides of each other that we won't have seen before. Will the friendships and respect we have now endure six weeks of close living and the tension of living on the edge for that length of time? The truth is, we don't know this for sure. Over the two weeks we gained some valuable insights into how we each make decisions and how we operate as a team. Or how we don't, as the case was once when we formed a plan, then each headed in three different directions! We found humour in disaster, like Graham's attempt to add a bit of flavour to the porridge by adding a cup of seawater. We found companionship in misery, when we got stitched up by a couple of fishermen who put us onto a 'primo camp site' and we slept the night under a leaky railway tarp on a platform, brittle with rot, that gradually collapsed throughout the night.

Although it wasn't easy, the friends forced themselves to confront and talk through personal issues that came up. 'On our way from Fiordland to Mount Cook's Tasman Lake, Graham's van blew up in Queenstown,' Marcus said. 'This caused some angst over money, and it meant we had to hire a car to go to Mount Cook. The team wasn't happy, in particular Graham. It would have been easy to pretend the "bad scene" hadn't happened, but we forced ourselves to talk about it. I think in some ways that gave us confidence to raise thorny issues [later].'

The lake at the terminal of the Tasman Glacier in Aoraki/Mount Cook National Park, New Zealand, proved to be an excellent location to test systems and equipment.

It had taken three years, but their preparation was almost complete. A few details remained. Marcus learned acupuncture in order to tend to Jonesy's back if necessary. Jonesy completed a boat master's qualification because although the three were experienced in the outdoors, none of them had much experience of the marine environment with its tides and currents. In mid-December 2000, Graham and the three Polar Bear kayaks boarded a plane for the southern port town of Ushuaia, Argentina. Two days before Christmas, Jonesy and Marcus followed.

Ushuaia, the world's southernmost city, huddles beneath the snowy peaks of the Martial Mountains. It is close enough to the Antarctic for a phone call to be local, but it is separated from the southern continent by one of the world's most ferocious stretches of water, the Drake Passage. In Ushuaia, the boys made friends easily despite the fact they knew little more than a few Spanish words. Their kayaks were a novelty and taking the locals kayaking was a good trading commodity for favours owed.

'The port is busy with tour ships heading to Antarctica and every day the town is swamped with many different nationalities,' Graham emailed from Ushuaia.

Great to meet the community of sailors and operators here who are passionate about Antarctica. We are slowly building a better picture of the weather and coastline features from these accommodating skippers. The best news to date is that it seems to be a good ice year. All skippers are reporting clear ice conditions through all the narrow passages right as far as the Polar Circle.

Sir Peter Blake and *Seamaster* planned to depart on 11 January. There was a lot to do: readying equipment, testing gear, learning the finer points of operating digital video cameras and how to shoot a documentary, organising a food cache for *Tooluka* to drop – and the on-going attempt to fill in the vast gaps in knowledge of the coastline.

One evening Jonesy visited a yacht called *Golden Fleece* and spoke with its skipper, reputed to have enormous experience of the less-travelled areas about which they were seeking information. Jonesy drank red wine with him and pored over the maps. He drew in some landing spots, but more often than not the marks drawn turned out to be ice towering above the water. Jonesy had this to say in his diary:

Jerome spoke of the difficulty of what we wished to do, without saying it was impossible. He spoke of the density of the wind and the sea. He spoke of wind rivers, all day katabatics, blower bays, deflection zones and big swells, not to mention the ice. I suddenly

The Argentinian city of Ushuaia, nestled between the Martial Mountains and the Beagle Channel, is the southernmost city in the world and the departure point for most expeditions to the Antarctic Peninsula.

understood the extreme nature of what we had set ourselves and why it has not been attempted before. He asked of our experience for such a trip. It was difficult to answer directly.

Ready or not, however, it was time to go. At sea, Antarctica arrives abruptly. Undulating between latitudes 50° and 60° South, there is a definite line where the sea surrounding Antarctica dips beneath the warmer oceans of the rest of the world. The temperature drops and fogs rise. The sea becomes less salty and colder from melting ice. A boat lying across the Antarctic Convergence can register a difference of temperature between bow and stern. It was in the small hours of 13 January 2001 that *Seamaster* crossed this line.

Marcus wrote:

The late Sir Peter Blake's flagship *Seamaster*, moored in Ushuaia before departing for the Antarctic Peninsula.

Gone are the hourglass dolphins, the floating albatross, the misty blue sea. The water is now a darker green, duller, colder. We are closer to the Pole – we are now in Antarctic waters. The Drake Passage raised hardly a hint of protest at our passing. 'The Drake Pond,' we quipped, though not too loudly. Like Viking raiders in the mist, we crept up on Antarctica. An iceberg appeared like a floating castle as we approached Ridley Island in the South Shetlands. The ocean had licked beautiful grooves around its midriff and it sat quite still in the water, as do all large icebergs, undisturbed by the motion of the waves. It could have been a shard of white land rising up from the seabed. Humpback whales, porpoising penguins, and even a demon leopard seal swam along side the boat. It was still calm and the fog burnt off in the afternoon sun. The Seamaster *moored for the night in Admiralty Bay on the east coast of King George Island. The northern end of the Antarctic Peninsula lay only 80 miles [130 kilometres] to the east.*

At 3am I woke with a start; boots thudded urgently on the deck, the motor shuddered to life and the anchor chain started clanking through the winch. Out of nowhere, a 90-knot wind was howling in the rigging and swinging the Seamaster *like a rag doll on the end of its mooring. The crew scrambled to escape our now-dangerous shallow anchorage and retreat to the safety of deeper water. The sense of comfort we'd gained from the previous day's pleasant conditions evaporated. This place, I realised, could dismiss us with a sneeze, with a flick of a humpback's tail.*

The speed and ferocity with which the wind emerged was sobering. Concerned that the tent would not withstand a gale, in the morning the team begged some sailcloth to reinforce the nylon guy valances. With some cautious to-ing and fro-ing *Seamaster* picked her way into the Antarctic Sound, or 'Iceberg Alley', where the behemoths of Antarctica – the huge, flat-topped tabular bergs broken off the Weddell Ice Shelf – drift westward in the sea currents.

In his final email from the Argentinian research base in Hope Bay, Graham wrote:

> *The adventure starts here. This is what we have dreamed of for a long time, and the look on Marcus and Jonesy's faces last night when the cloud lifted and the sun shone on the mountains around Hope Bay was worth all the effort so far…*
>
> *I am so happy to be back on the frozen land and on our own terms, our own rules and common sense.*
>
> *Into the cold mist.*
>
> *Graham*

The crew of *Seamaster* struggle with an early morning gale that erupted
while moored in Admiralty Bay, King George Island.

Capitán Arturo Prat (Chile)

Byers Peninsula

Livingston I.

Byth Point

Snow I.

Deception I.

Port Foster

Neptunes Bellows

Bransfield Strait

Low I.

Cape Garry

Gourdin I.

Antarctic Sound

Astrolabe I.

Cape Legoupil

Huon Bay

General Bernardo O'Higgins (Chile)

Cape Ducorps

Mott Snowfield

Tabarin Peninsula

Hope Bay

Lafond Bay

Cockerell Peninsula

Esperanza (Argentina)

Marescot Point

Cape Roquemaurel

Loius-Philippe Plateau

Duse Bay

Brown Bluff 2444 m

Bone Bay

Trinity Peninsula

Eyrie Bay

Tower I.

Cape Neumayer

Cape Kjellman

Gavin Ice Piedmont

Russell West Glacier

Cugnot Ice Piedmont

Beak I.

Tail I.

Eagle I.

Milburn Bay

Charcot Bay

Egg I.

Corry I.

Hoseason I.

Trinity I.

Cape Kater

Vega I.

Christiania Is.

Lancaster Bay

McNeile Glacier

Long I.

Prince Gustav Channel

Intercurrence I.

Skottsberg Point

Orléans Strait

Whittle Peninsula

Whitecloud Glacier

Herbert Sound

Erebus and Terror Gulf

Liège I.

Cape Andreas

Curtiss Bay

Temple Glacier

Ulu Peninsula

Croft Bay

Bouquet Bay

Macleod Point

Cape Herschel

Havilland Point

Davis Coast

Two Hummock I.

Hill Bay

Mitchell Point

Sterneck I.

Detroit Plateau

Mt Haddington 1630 m

Lecointe I.

Hughes Bay

Hunt I.

Graham Passage

Bluff I.

Salvesen Cove

Tournachon Peak 858 m

James Ross I.

Eckener Point

Blériot Glacier

Mt Zeppelin 1265 m

Wellman Glacier

Cape Longing

Snow Hill I.

Gerlache Strait

Ross Cove

Charlotte Bay

Enterprise I.

Nansen I.

Nobile Glacier

Danco Coast

Antarctic Peninsula

Nordenskjöld Coast

Larsen Inlet

Admiralty Sound

Brooklyn I.

Renard Glacier

Larsen Ice Shelf

Cape Garry

0 10 25 30 40 50 60

Kilometres

From Hope to Enterprise

Marcus Waters

The day was bleak. At the northern tip of the Antarctic Peninsula, low cloud spat drizzle and snow onto the ice, rock and sea of Hope Bay. At the far end of the bay, a steep, crevassed glacier plunged into the water. Impregnable ice cliffs guarded the rest of the bay, apart from the flat rock and gravel where the Argentinian Esperanza Base sat. Across the sound, the rounded bulk of Joinville Island appeared and disappeared in the mist.

I wanted to get going. In spite of the Argentinians' radio forecast for more inclement weather, I was both eager and anxious to find out what we had got ourselves into. To be master of your own fate is a privilege few people experience in the Antarctic. Yet here I was, launching my kayak into the near-freezing sea, unguided by anyone else's advice, answerable only to my two friends and my own good judgement. I caught Graham and Jonesy's first Antarctic paddle strokes on videotape, hurried to my boat, brushed the snow off my seat and pushed away from land.

The first 200 kilometres of our journey would be critical. With almost no shelter from offshore islands, the swells and storms of the Drake Passage smash unhindered into the coast. In order to move quickly through this exposed section we had opted for a food cache further down the coast. With less food and lighter boats we hoped to sneak past Antarctica's northern snout unscathed.

Droves of penguins porpoised towards our kayaks as we paddled. Seals emerged from the deep, clearing their noses with puffs and snorts. The waters of Hope Bay were seething with life intent on completing the season's cycle before being forced north to warmer climes by winter. Among the floating ice, the fins of two orca broke the surface. Jonesy, Graham and I grouped together nervously, seeking safety in numbers, and paddled for open water.

The coastline was an unbroken 15- to 70-metre wall of ice – beautiful, like cracked marble. Centuries-old dust lines that had once been the snow surface wrinkled the ice face. From the top of the cliffs, unmarred by rock or mountain, the Mott Snowfield receded smoothly into the hinterland. Calving ice

Hope Bay at the northern tip of the Peninsula, was the starting point of our journey. Many hard winters were spent here during the Heroic Age of Antarctic exploration between 1901 and 1910, and Nordenskjöld's stone hut still remains from this period.

cliffs boomed, submitting another lump of ice to the sea to begin its doomed life as an iceberg. There was no getting out of our kayaks. Wind and snow whipped us. Visibility came and went.

I felt dwarfed by the enormousness of our surroundings: the immense glaciers, the vast snowfield sweeping into the snowbound interior of the Antarctic Peninsula. I glanced down at our laminated map. At home in his lounge in Auckland, Jonesy had scrawled gaily in the margin: 'Very strong katabatic winds blow down Hope Bay with little warning'. Those words now had meaning and we each began glancing anxiously inland for worsening weather. Katabatics can accelerate to more than 160 kilometres per hour within minutes. If we were caught by such a gale in the middle of a long bay crossing, we would be in deep trouble. Like stalked prey, we constantly looked over our shoulders, watching the clouds, sneaking from refuge to refuge.

Fully enveloped by Antarctic mist, I pulled up the large hood on my paddle jacket. Snow gathered on our backs as a surging, dark two-metre sea shunted us around. I said a silent thanks to Steve Gurney who designed our pogies. Without these closed-cell foam gloves, our hands would have been frozen and useless in minutes. Muffled as we were, it was an effort to keep within speaking distance, but we had to stay together. In wind and a sloppy sea it would be easy to be separated. Here on the coast of the Antarctic Peninsula, I was connected by more than friendship: there was an invisible lifeline between us. Should any of us break it, we'd be sunk.

Much of our plan for the days ahead was based on a wing and a prayer, a hope that we would find somewhere to land each day. Coastal information for the northern end of the Peninsula was particularly sketchy. These waters receive little shipping and virtually no cruise or charter boats. Nevertheless, we had seen

No more practice, no more 'what ifs' – Marcus confronts the sobering reality of Antarctica's wet and cold.

Leaving Hope Bay – not a coastal holiday location.

research that documented a penguin rookery on Gourdin Island, 30 kilometres from Hope Bay. We figured if penguins could get out of the water, so could we.

After four hours paddling I started to become concerned: we should have been able to see Gourdin Island, but there was nothing. We edged closer to the coast to inspect a cove for a possible landing, but the broken jumble of ice blocks beneath the sheer ice cliff and the breaking swell made landing impossible. Thoughts of incorrect maps began to play on my mind. Back in the safety of New Zealand, we had programmed the co-ordinates of various milestones into our GPS. Yet, contrary to the GPS's opinion that we were sitting in the middle of Gourdin Island, we were still very much surrounded by water. Over the next few days we discovered that the maps, though accurate, were often about 800 metres out of kilter, but now I was worried. It was midnight. There was nothing we could do but keep paddling.

Slowly a dark pyramid emerged from the mist. As we approached we could see swell breaking on the coastline, a dangerous landing proposition for our 80-kilogram boats. Changing course, we headed for a small cove on the sheltered western side of the island.

First into the cove, Jonesy yelled to us that a metre-high snow berm would make getting out difficult, but possible. I'd always attributed Jonesy's great balance to wide feet, but as he landed his unstable kayak smoothly on a small rock I figured there was more to his equilibrium than splayed toes. Jonesy hauled his boat up onto the snow and returned to help Graham and me with the difficult task of getting our kayaks out of the water. He grabbed the bow loop on my kayak and heaved with all his might. Graham and I howled as the rudder on my kayak caught the back of Graham's boat, but too late. I looked at my bent rudder, annoyed at the need for a repair already. In a tense silence we finished securing all three kayaks on the snow. With the application of a little care, I thought to myself, it was unnecessary to break things, unnecessary to jeopardise the expedition with wrecked equipment. The others broke my reverie, yelling at me to get the tent out of my boat.

By chance we'd found a perfect spot. The island sheltered us from the northeast wind and a small pile of rocks offered protection from the south. At 1.30am we finally crawled into our sleeping bags in our first Antarctic camp. The tent rattled with wind and sleet. I fell asleep wondering what deep breaths might be summoned from the lungs of the interior.

We awoke to another grim day. Rain and bouts of snow lashed the tent and a 15-knot southerly head wind would mean heavy paddling. The wind had filled our small cove with blocks of ice and thick brash, and even if we'd been desperate escaping to open water would be difficult. We stayed where we were.

Our sheltered camp spot was a coveted piece of ground. During the night a giant crabeater seal had wriggled ashore and fallen asleep a few metres from our tent door. He and his kind had obviously been doing this for generations as seal hair and dung coated the rocks and snow. Gourdin Island was also alive with gentoo and Adelie penguins. From rookeries above our camp they dutifully and comically waddled past our tent to the ocean for food or lugged their bellies, heavy with fish, back uphill to feed their brood. The penguins ignored us, totally absorbed in feeding their young. There was regurgitated krill and poop everywhere; the

Orca were surprisingly cautious, staying away from our kayaks.

39

round fluffy chicks were being reared in it like bacteria in agar jelly.

As we spooned up our breakfast, a procession of four gentoo penguins waddled by. The first in line walked straight into a guy rope, presumably the first he'd ever encountered, and fell flat on his face. The second penguin made the same mistake, while his companion, having righted himself, was now being tripped up on a second guy rope. This continued until all four penguins were squawking on the ground, dignity in tatters, bewildered by the strange obstacles.

Gentoo penguin chicks, the comedians of our Antarctic summer.

Once thought to hold significant evolutionary secrets, penguins have fascinated humans for decades. A party on Captain Scott's 1911 *Terra Nova* expedition embarked on a 96-kilometre midwinter sledge trip in freezing temperatures to collect penguin eggs from Cape Crozier. This went down in history as "the worst journey in the world" and few since have challenged it for the title.

During the day the weather cleared and I climbed the scree to a small saddle in the middle of the island to survey our new environment. To the north, giant tabular bergs crept out of the Antarctic Sound between Hope Bay and Joinville Island. As large as football fields, these flat-topped icebergs had broken off the Weddell Ice Shelf and were now drifting into the Drake Passage. To the south, the Peninsula disappeared into the wind and mist. The small sanctuary of our yellow tent looked inadequate and lonely in this vast seascape of white and grey. We were alone with the penguins and seals.

Everything was so new: the ice, the weather, the wildlife. Strong southerly winds whitened the wave tops and clogged our bay with big ice blocks grinding against each other like apples in a water barrel. We were effectively trapped. Yet I felt that, simply by being there, I was absorbing the messages of the environment, learning the lessons of Antarctica, and was thus content to wait another two nights for better weather. I felt we were wise to ease into it.

On the other side of the island a mass of brash ice shimmered like jewels in the afternoon sunlight, creating the illusion of solidity. Waves rippled through the ice and then tinkled to a stop on the rocky beach. The penguins hopped across the brash or flopped onto their bellies, wriggling like spiders until there was a hole in the ice through which they could dive. Then word seemed to get out that smart penguins could reach the sea and avoid the difficult ice surface via a small two-metre-high point at the far

Large icebergs often become grounded and may spend years in one spot. We paddled through this 'graveyard' near Pléneau Island.
Overleaf: When your vision is clear, decision-making is easy – through two years of dreaming and planning we held fast to a vision like this.

end of the bay, and a line of birds scurried off to check it out. A volley of squawking, jostling, retreating and advancing ensued as they weighed the pros and cons of the leap. Eventually a brave penguin made the jump and splashed into the surging sea. The others peered down, then followed with varying degrees of confidence. A few shook their black and white heads and traipsed back inland – a fascinating display of team decision-making.

It made me deliriously happy to feel some sun and enjoy the island and its inhabitants. I live in a country where any animal without a collar or ear tag will bolt from humans. It was humbling to be surrounded by wildlife that did not care whether I existed or not. I sat and watched; among those penguins I felt uniquely connected to nature, to the powerful life force that drives creatures to replicate themselves.

It felt peculiar to pull your drinking water out of the sea, but the brash ice made far better drinking water than the seal-fouled snow around the tent. I piled lumps of ice by the tent ready for the pot, unaware that the ice block would attract all seal hair in the immediate vicinity. Inevitably the coarse fibres made their way into our cooking water, our tea, our cups, only to be filtered out by our teeth.

We woke early to a clear, still morning, but we weren't out of the woods yet. While the ice in our small alcove had dispersed, there were still some major blocks jostling for limited space. Between the rock entrance and the ice lay a narrow corridor through which we might be able to squeeze and escape to open water, but it was a moving target. The swell surged and the ice bashed into the rock, sealing the exit, then opening up again as the wave receded. If we mistimed our run we would be crushed between the rock and the ice.

I lined up for the narrow gap between the rock and ice and powered into the ocean unscathed, only to find I couldn't drop my rudder all the way into the water. Jonesy's fix-it job hadn't worked. I'd have to run the gap a second time, haul my kayak out of the water and fix the rudder. I've always taken care of my gear and enjoy the ritual of cleaning and maintaining my equipment before putting it away for the next adventure. Few things annoy me more than gear failure in the outdoors. I tried to put on a brave face, attempting the 'she'll be right' demeanour and rugged confidence of the handyman.

On the open sea it was warm and calm. Lumps of brash shone and crackled in the sunlight. The grey of the previous few days was gone and we were left with a vivid blue sea and sky. It was beautiful, the sea harmlessly slapping about our boats. Here, on the northern end of the Peninsula, the terrain was gentle, with mountains that were little more than rounded mounds of snow. The broad snowfields, punctuated by a few sharp nunataks, finished in 30-metre coastal ice cliffs. The great Bransfield Strait extended to our right and beyond the horizon the South Shetlands. 'There's *nowhere* else in the world I would rather be!', exclaimed Graham with typical exuberance. We came across our first open water icefield, a narrow band of brash stretching like a ribbon perpendicular to our direction. Tentatively we negotiated ice blocks ranging in size from footballs to car engines. Edging our boats carefully into the ice, we discovered the blocks would move when we hit them: yes, we could pole them out of the way with our paddles.

In the distance, whales broke the calm surface, expelling great lungfuls of air and then gently slipping back beneath the waves. They followed a similar path to our own and came within 50 metres of our kayaks before disappearing.

Suddenly, there appeared round the corner a black Zodiac inflatable full of people. The travellers waved at us, we waved back, they buzzed around us, inching a little closer. We knew we were close to the Chilean military base General Bernardo O'Higgins, so we were more of a shock to them than they were to us. Someone yelled something Spanish at us.

'Hola,' we replied.

An English speaker called, 'Where are you from?'

'New Zealand,' we yelled back.

This obviously made no more sense than three people appearing out of nowhere paddling sea kayaks. After general confusion they established that we were not some Argentinian attack force sneaking up on them and gestured at us to follow them.

Early in our planning stages of the expedition we had debated the value of attempting to complete the traverse of the Antarctic Peninsula unaided. This would have meant travelling from Hope Bay to the Antarctic Circle without a food dump, without calling at any of the research bases along the way and without accepting so much as a cup of tea from anyone. We admired the nobility of the concept, but doubted the practicality. For one

Scanning for open leads in the brash ice.

thing, we simply could not safely carry the required weight of food and technical equipment for a month-long kayak expedition in the Antarctic. Although our sea kayaks were large enough to carry the stores, we needed to be able to paddle them for unknown distances and remain strong enough to handle a difficult wind or sea at the end of a long day. There was also the question of whether we would have to drag our sea kayaks across any sea ice. Hence we had opted for a food cache and dispensed with the purist notion of no outside contact or assistance. In hindsight this was an excellent choice: we would have missed a very colourful part of our adventure had we ignored the bases and their inhabitants.

It took a while for the Chilean Captain Wouter to comprehend what we were doing, but when he'd grasped the concept, in a hugely animated fashion, he insisted we follow him up to their base. Our boats were whisked out of the sea and passed up a chain of soldiers that had formed behind us.

Sounds of humanity and machinery assaulted us. Within 10 minutes of feeling utterly alone in

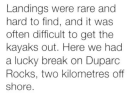

Landings were rare and hard to find, and it was often difficult to get the kayaks out. Here we had a lucky break on Duparc Rocks, two kilometres off shore.

Antarctica, we were sitting in the officers' mess giggling at the incongruity. Pictures of Pinochet and various military coats of arms adorned the walls. Captain Wouter appeared with three plates of steak: 'Eat, eat…you take us by surprise!' We were invited to stay for the night, but I wanted to go. It was nice to meet the Chileans, yet already I missed the simplicity of our camp and the ease of our discussion. As politely as we could we told our hosts we had to take advantage of the good weather, and once more our heavy boats were passed down a chain of soldiers and back onto the water. The Chileans snapped photos of us and wished us luck.

Ten kilometres away, on the south side of Cockerell Peninsula, we found a small cove and an easy exit point onto a raised beach inhabited by seals. We clambered out of our boats and claimed a piece of shore for the humans. The seals protested then reluctantly agreed that we could probably share their hair- and dung-covered stones. We shovelled a bit of snow to make a slightly cleaner and more comfortable sleeping platform. It had been a glorious blue-sky day, with little wind. We sat, chatted and prepared dinner, in good spirits.

I find early starts difficult but my compadres are early birds and after what seemed like just minutes of sleep, I was passed our morning fare of porridge fortified with protein powder. On the other side of our cove, water poured in a neat waterfall from the snow pack. Running water meant we did not have to melt ice and Jonesy paddled across to fill billies and water bottles.

With a mysterious cloud veil in the west, we watched the sky during breakfast and guessed it was safe to continue. We still couldn't identify any clues the weather might be giving. The previous day we'd heard more katabatic wind stories from the Chileans – tales of billowing clouds seeping down from the snow-fields and rapidly filling the air with tremendous gusts. It was enough to make the most gung-ho sea kayaker pause in the morning. I didn't want to become a rescue mission; I wanted success, but not at any price. I wanted to be able to go home knowing our own competence and decision-making had seen us through, that we'd adventured well. These sentiments were to come back to haunt us in a few weeks time.

We set off in calm conditions, heading for a rocky promontory in the distance. It seemed an age away as I wistfully calculated that I could cover the same distance in 50 minutes in the light racing kayak hanging in my garage at home. Water passed under our boats and eventually we were gazing up at the rock bluffs. But there was no stopping here. The coastline was a continuous ice cliff, sheer and dangerous, promising no landings.

We fixed our gaze on the next headland. By late afternoon, we'd been in our boats for more than eight hours, and an unbroken ice cliff stretched all the way down to the precipitous rock buttress of Cape

Roquemaurel. We were tired and the dull realisation that we might have to spend the night in our kayaks began to gnaw away at my consciousness. It's hard to sleep in a kayak. Almost all your weight rests on your pelvic bones, giving you a very numb and sore bum, as many an occasional overnight kayaker will testify. I had taken considerable time before the expedition padding out my kayak seat. It had taken me numerous pieces of closed-cell foam, a rasp, sandpaper and endless tinkering to get my seat comfortable. Nevertheless, the thought of spending a full night in the kayak in damp clothes, moving constantly for warmth, was not appealing.

Our only hope was the Duparc Rocks, a small set of islands two kilometres off the coast. The closer we got the less likely they looked: just dollops of snow-covered rock too steep for landing. After circling the larger island we found a thin cleft, a break in the rock with the tide swilling in and out. The narrow entrance was only two metres wide and with the swell it was going to be a tricky landing. Nervously we hovered, then, like lemmings, we went for it, running the narrow gap and driving the boats up onto a rock at the end of the channel. We jumped quickly out of the kayaks before we could be sucked back by the waves.

The proposed camp spot was just big enough for our tent, with snow-covered rocks like battlements on either side, and two seals, one dead, one alive. We were about 15 metres above the water and it felt like our own tiny castle.

The Antarctic coastline stretched north and south before us. The cold grey sea formed a moat between our island and the advancing snow slopes of the mainland. The mountains had lost their sleek baby look and were becoming higher and steeper. To the south, the towering rock of Cape Roquemaurel broke through

The luxuries of civilization satisfy only those wants which they themselves create.
Apsley Cherry-Garrard, 1911, Hut Point, Antarctica

the ice cliffs like a face with a protruding forehead and deep-set eyes. It wore a sinister frown, maybe at the thought of our passing. It was a spectacular camp. I became quite animated, grabbing the video camera and demanding interviews from the other two. The tension of the afternoon evaporated and we happily brewed our soup.

It was an overcast morning as we set out, with dull clouds and little to distinguish between the sea and the sky – Antarctic grey, we called it. The face-like features of Cape Roquemaurel dissolved into the rock's elements as we passed and headed into our first major bay crossing where we would be exposed to the whim of katabatics. At the far side of Bone Bay rose a tall rock with a cupola of smooth snow on top like a badly fitting wig. Our kayaks sliced through the sea surface, creating ripples and folds in the satiny water. I concentrated on my paddling technique, trying to place the blade in the optimum position, pulling it through the water, setting up for the next paddle stroke. It added some degree of intellectual stimulation to the physical swinging of the blade. Across the bay, protected by several grounded icebergs, a rocky low-tide beach at the base of a cliff offered rest. A small cave offered protection from the rocks and pebbles that bounced down the cliff.

Jonesy looked unhappy and withdrawn. I began to wonder what Graham or I had done to cause this bad mood. After gently angling around the subject it transpired Jonesy's back was causing him grief. Just before our departure from Auckland Jonesy had taken me along to his physiotherapist for a crash course on acupuncture. I'd learnt how to relieve some of the tension in his trapezius using needles. There was, however, some risk in this strategy: if I got the needles in the wrong place I could puncture his lung.

Jonesy was in pain and wanted to camp as soon as possible, but high tide would soon have waves washing at the base of the cliff. After tea and applications of the anti-inflammatory cream Voltaren, we launched the boats to look for a camp. It was fruitless. With no landing spot in sight, we found ourselves committed to a long, exposed crossing of Charcot Bay.

The bay is a classic blower, a 20-kilometre-wide break in the coast, that breathed katabatics. It would take us four hours to cross, during which time we'd be very exposed. Charcot Bay represented a mental milestone for us. New Zealand's Antarctic veteran Colin Monteath had promised that once past Charcot Bay, we'd gain some shelter from the Peninsula's offshore islands. In the distance on the far side of the bay lay Whittle Peninsula. It was still, the sea was oily calm, Antarctic grey surrounded us. The bay was more than 16 kilometres deep. Large glaciers receded into the hinterland and steep mountains rose from the crevassed snowfields. This magnificent scenery effortlessly measured up to the majesty and splendour I had held in my mind's eye for so long. Looking apprehensively across my left shoulder for tell-tale signs of

The four-hour open crossing of Charcot Bay was very stressful, as we were exposed to a potentially lethal katabatic wind.

katabatic wind, I swung into the crossing.

What does one think about during these long crossings? It was with interest that I had read, in his book *Ice Trek*, of the erotic thoughts Eric Phillips had during the long days of his sledge trek to the South Pole. With slowly changing scenery and a repetitive paddling action, I certainly found some entertainment in such thoughts. I also thought about the future, my partner Erin and contemplated my past musical career. Intermittently, I looked over my shoulder for a change in the weather, a riffle on the sea that might indicate wind whistling down from the Detroit Plateau to send us tumbling out into the Bransfield Strait.

Through murky evening light and falling snow I began to see the collapsed rock formations and surging cliffline of Whittle Peninsula. Graham had picked up the pace in the last half hour, presumably expecting to find a place to land, but he now looked miffed. The cliffs boomed and echoed with the grandeur of a cathedral, waves exploded into thick spray on the rocks. Obviously, there was no stopping here. There was no option but to carry on.

As I trailed behind the other two, I noticed that, inexplicably, they seemed to be cutting a tight line between the coastal rocks and a large iceberg. Why had they chosen that route, I wondered? I could see waves breaking on a shallow shoal ahead of me, but figured I could sneak between them. Suddenly a wave erupted into three metres of white foam beside me. Instinctively I leaned forward and braced. The wave poured over my head and effortlessly swept my boat sideways. It dissipated as quickly as it had emerged, but then from nowhere another exploded and covered me in more breathtaking icy froth. I paddled hard, loaded with adrenaline. As I surfed out of the waves and caught my breath, I saw that the ice axe on my front deck had come loose of its bungy cord. As I reached for it, the axe slipped into the water, its white shaft shining as it disappeared into the deep. I was annoyed at losing the axe and I felt stupid. Capsizing in breaking waves and freezing water would have been exceptionally ugly and dangerous. Jonesy and Graham sidled up, questioning what the heck I had been doing. It was late and we were tired. With a sense of urgency we paddled on, desperate to escape from the sea.

Our camp on the Whittle Peninsula was a forbidding place, but welcome after a 16-hour paddle.

Finally, deep in a small cove surrounded by huge 150-metre hanging ice cliffs, we found a snow slope that descended into the sea fringed by a rocky beach. Broken rock and debris lay on the snow. It was a forbidding place, but after 16 hours and 65 kilometres in our kayaks we didn't care. With dead legs we grovelled onto the rocky beach, then up to a large flat area, sinking up to our thighs in soft snow.

'Do you think we should camp as high up the snow bank as we can, in case of ice collapse and a large wave washing up?' I asked the others. We moved inland a little more, but the desire to sleep on flat ground kept us from climbing too high. We floundered in the deep snow until the tent was erected. Despite my tiredness I didn't sleep well. My sleeping bag was damp. I lay clammy and chilled, turning restlessly with crossed arms, trying to stay warm.

This was a wild place and I felt like a lost bug. Icebergs and a confetti of brash floated in the bay. Looming cliffs dwarfed us, rising straight out of the water and soaring up to the high snowfields of the Whittle Peninsula. At the end of the bay, some 800 metres from our camp, a vast column of ice towered high into the air, held in space by some mysterious force.

As the day warmed into the afternoon, ice began to melt from the cliffs until a ceaseless stream of snow and debris poured from the heights, like a waterfall. We wandered to the edge of the bouldery beach, sensing that something was about to happen, and stood there cameras in hand. The tide was out, leaving a five-metre berm. Suddenly, at the end of the bay, the colossal column of ice crumbled. With a deafening roar it exploded into an 80-metre-wide wave of ice blocks, debris and powder. Thousands of tonnes of ice plummeted into the sea, throwing up spray and clouds of ice.

The sheer magnitude was terrifying.

In the middle of the bay a wave grew like a giant fold in a silky sheet. At the beach edge the water was sucked into the belly of this forming monster. Realising we were in trouble, I turned and started to run. Graham scampered in front of me. I lost sight of Jonesy as I floundered through the deep snow, tripped and fell face first. The wave crashed over the top of the beach-head and raced up behind us, bubbling and seething. In a panic I pushed myself out of the snow and seal dung and carried on running, past our tent

We cheered and clapped as a huge column of ice broke off and plunged into the sea – until we saw the resulting wave surging up the bay towards our camp.

Though the prevailing nor'east winds were usually on our tail, they carried rain, sleet and snow.

and up the snow slope. Two metres from our tent and kayaks the wave gave up the chase: its white fingers hissed, died and slithered back to sea.

We'd come as close as a seal's whisker to disaster. A couple more metres and the wave would have claimed our tent, our boats and all our gear. Graham was ahead of me and I could see Jonesy further along the snow slope. Panting, I let out a squeaky string of expletives and giggled hysterically. Miraculously our gear was still intact. The worst that had happened was one wet boot, which came off Jonesy's foot as he fled and then, amazingly, washed up in the wave behind him. It felt as if the sleeping giant Antarctica had rolled over and murmured in its sleep. What would happen if this behemoth ever woke up?

It was a tense night, listening to the ice cliffs above us, praying for the temperature to cool, a refreezing that would stop more collapses. Little bugs don't live long in Antarctica.

I woke to find I hadn't died during the night. It was another Antarctic grey day, with the smell of snow and sleet in the air. With some trepidation we paddled off towards Lancaster Bay, our next exposed bay crossing.

The weather was foul by the time we were committed to Lancaster Bay. Snow and sleet blew on our backs and the sea had picked up to a three-metre swell. We were enveloped by the Antarctic grey, sightless and completely reliant on the compass for navigation. Breaking waves poured pillows of white foam around my midriff. In warmer climes, with sun, a weather forecast and a known destination, the waves would have been fun. Here the stormy conditions and 50-metre visibility made me anxious. Hoods up, we paddled grimly on, riding the slop and bracing into the waves.

Forty-five kilometres later we passed the craggy, lofty Cape Andreas. All afternoon I'd clung to a hope that this would offer a haven, but as we wobbled about in the confusion of swell and reflected waves I was disappointed. We'd been paddling for 10 hours. For the first time on the expedition I was feeling really down. We'd been buffeted all day by the weather. We were wet and cold from the breaking waves, and now I had to contend with squalls and williwaws blowing snow in my face. I desperately wanted to stop. Disheartened I paddled ahead of the others, scouring the shore for a landing spot. After five kilometres, I whooped with relief after spying a small flat peninsula with a sheltered beach full of brash ice.

We were another 50 kilometres closer to the Antarctic Circle, but the heavy boats, long days and the cold wetness were taking their toll. Everything was damp, my aching muscles and tendons were feeling the strain, red wear marks and blisters had formed on my hands. In near silence we went about our camp chores. In my diary I wrote: 'This is very committing.'

Jonesy was experiencing shoulder pain again. There were major knots in his back around the shoulder blade and with my thumbs I rubbed them out, as his chiropractor had taught me. Despite the damp it was a wonderful sleep – the most glorious reward, more pure than praise, more honest than money.

We each carried a thermos for a hot drink on the long, cold days.

As fate would have it, the following day I strained my own lower back. I'd done this before, tearing ligaments around the base of my spine which reduced me to a hobbling grump. It wasn't so much the pain that bothered me as the thought of letting Graham and Jonesy down, or the inability to respond with appropriate strength and speed during a crucial moment. Fortunately I could sit in my kayak and paddle, but lifting our heavy kayaks in and out of the water was impossible. Now there were two of us dipping into the Voltaren supplies. Our day-to-day lives back in New Zealand, especially mine as an office-dwelling management consultant, certainly didn't involve the rigours we were now putting our bodies through. Strained backs were a hazard we had been worried about before we left. We'd put in considerable time trying to invent a system that would make carrying the boats easier and safer, but in the end had come up with nothing.

With no chance to dry anything, life in the tent became progressively wetter, and smellier.

We spent the day in the tent. It was raining, grey and miserable. I'd been under the misguided impression that it did not rain in Antarctica. Now, I can categorically say that it certainly does rain on the Antarctic Peninsula. Rain is the worst of the elements. You can protect yourself against wind, snow, cold but not rain. Rain soaked the tent, melted the snow around the tent entrance and made it impossible to move without getting wet. Once our clothes were wet it was impossible to dry them, and apart from our damp paddling gear, we had little wet-weather clothing. There wasn't much to do other than lie in the tent and try to avoid getting our sleeping bags wet against the tent walls. We drank tea and read the books we'd rationed ourselves. Graham listened to his Walkman, a luxury Jonesy and I thought decadent.

During the afternoon the rain petered out. Sinking up to our knees in the granulated snow, we wove a path to the high point of our peninsula. Our spit was a good anchorage and on top we discovered a collapsed tripod that must have been a beacon to boats. It was a sign that we were moving into the middle section of the Antarctic Peninsula, where there was greater shelter from offshore islands, more boat traffic and the promise of more numerous landings.

All was grey as we crossed Curtiss Bay, but rounding the southern point we saw in the distance a colour we hadn't seen in days – the orange and brown of the Argentinian base, Primavera. It was a deserted ghost town of small huts joined by boardwalks. We pushed on towards the small Sprightly Island, where Roger Wallis had left our food cache. While we paddled, Roger was elsewhere on the Antarctic Peninsula

supporting another expedition: two Australian climbers who were trekking from Hope Bay along the spine of the Peninsula. Roger was to pick them up and take them back to Ushuaia before returning to the southern peninsula to rendezvous with us.

  Just the previous day, Roger had assured us via a crackling HF radio signal that Sprightly Island was always free of ice. As we drew closer a thick field of brash ice halted our travel. After consulting the map we decided the small dark dot in the distance was the island encased in ice. Searching for a way through, we paddled a couple of kilometres east, and then back to the west before finding a slight weakness where we barged our way through some of the thickest brash we'd encountered. We fell into single file, the leader finding the weaknesses and pushing smaller blocks out of the way with his paddle. After a few hours of

In the early part of our journey, we saw humpback whales on most days.

hard work we pulled around a rocky point and in a small alcove up a scree slope, just 50 metres away, lay a wooden box, incongruous in the wild landscape.

Between us and our food cache, the sea surged over large rocks. As we bobbed up and down in our kayaks it was difficult to tell if there was safe landing. Jonesy wanted to go for it, to ride over the rocks on an incoming wave and trust there was a beach beyond. I thought we should have lunch and see if a turn in tide changed the nature of the landing. Graham agreed and we paddled back to where we could get out. There was an uncomfortable silence as we hauled the kayaks onto our lunch rock. Jonesy wasn't talking. When Graham pressed him he expressed his frustration at our decision. He'd trained to pull off such difficult landings and thought if we timed it right we could do it safely. I couldn't understand it. It just seemed an unnecessary risk: why potentially damage the boats when a change in the tide may remove the problem altogether? We ate lunch and Jonesy wandered up the steep scree behind us. Graham and I shuffled around on the uncomfortable rocks, biding our time. After an hour Jonesy returned, cured by his short adventure. He reported an overland route to our cache was impossible and that the sea had now covered the threatening rocks; he also warned of a new hazard: aggressive dive-bombing skuas.

Because we were ahead of schedule, with plenty of supplies left, our rendezvous with our food cache was not the rapturous encounter Captain Scott would have had with his One Tonne Depot. Our problem was that with four weeks of new supplies, the kayaks would be heavier than when we started at Hope Bay. Having run our boats over the rocks into the still-surging cove, we decided to camp and spend the afternoon in bright sunshine sorting our provisions. As we prised the boxes open we came across the notes we had written to ourselves while packing the cache in Ushuaia. 'Go hard,' I'd scrawled in a fit of wisdom.

Cursing and straining, we launched our weighty boats the following morning. They sat noticeably lower in the water. We pushed through the brash ice that still surrounded Sprightly and escaped into Hughes Bay. We hadn't been paddling long when misty flumes erupted around the bay. Pods of humpback whales were trawling for krill. A whale surfaced metres from us, breathed a full bellows of air, then mysteriously sank below the surface. Jonesy grinned from ear to ear as the whale dived under his boat. Another was asleep, floating like a dark log on the surface. Occasionally it would breathe, sending a thin, foul mist of air wafting across the sea. Jonesy the hunter gleefully got in close for a photo. I held back, unsure of what a sleeping whale does when it wakes up. Eventually it did wake, but there was little commotion. The huge back arced, the wonderful tail rose out of the water and the whale disappeared into the deep.

I pulled ahead of the others and became lost in my own world, basking in the sunshine and

Icebergs come in a remarkable array of shapes and sizes and were a source of constant amazement.

Waves – the master carvers of icebergs.

marvelling at everything around me. After a few hours, we entered a narrow channel between the mainland and Murray Island, coincidentally named Graham Passage. The sheltered channel was mirror calm and alive with glorious reflections of the surrounding mountains.

As I emerged from the confines of the passage into the Gerlache Strait, it was as if I had stepped through a magic doorway to a vast frozen wonderland. The nose of my kayak, which had been slicing through the silken water, slowed and stopped as I ceased paddling and floated in awe. Before me the mountains soared higher, steeper and more magnificent than before, rising into the air like Norse gods and stretching south as far as the eye could see. The sun was so bright that the mountains shimmered in the haze. Colossal crevassed glaciers poured into the sea, wide and impenetrable, sweeping back for tens of kilometres to their smooth névés. Brabant Island lay to the right, the mainland to the left, and I could no longer see open ocean. It was huge, majestic, a frozen coast. The others caught up and we sat there, speechless.

It was mid-afternoon. Ahead of us lay the 16-kilometre-wide Charlotte Bay, the last big bay crossing until we became enveloped in the shelter of the mid-Peninsula islands. We'd done 45 kilometres already and Graham was keen to stop and photograph the sunset. But my approach had always been to push on whenever possible, to paddle up the kilometres as quickly as we could, especially when we could take advantage of kind weather. I was feeling good and even relished the thought of more paddling. My argument won the day, and we settled into our crossing, heading for Portal Point as the sun dipped below the horizon.

In the past, expeditions to explore the Peninsula hinterland have landed at Portal Point, and indeed, the snowfields offered an unchallenged route to the interior. In the expansive terrain, with a hazy light blue sky, I felt drawn to walk among the distant mountains myself, to experience the simple beauty of snow and rock. I began to understand how Antarctica could mesmerise people and why explorers felt compelled to haul laden sledges to the South Pole.

It had been the best day's sea kayaking of my life. We had broken the back of the first part of our expedition and would soon reach the relative sanctuary of the middle section, where landings were more common, and charter boats visited. The previous two weeks had seen us arrive in Antarctica, survive the first exposed crucial section and accustom our bodies to the work of paddling. I realised that I was no longer a total Antarctic 'newbie', not the same person who, a fortnight before, had taken his first tense paddle strokes at the northern tip of the Peninsula. We'd dipped our paddles in Antarctic waters, learned to respect the ways of the southern continent. I was starting to feel as if we'd earned our ticket to visit.

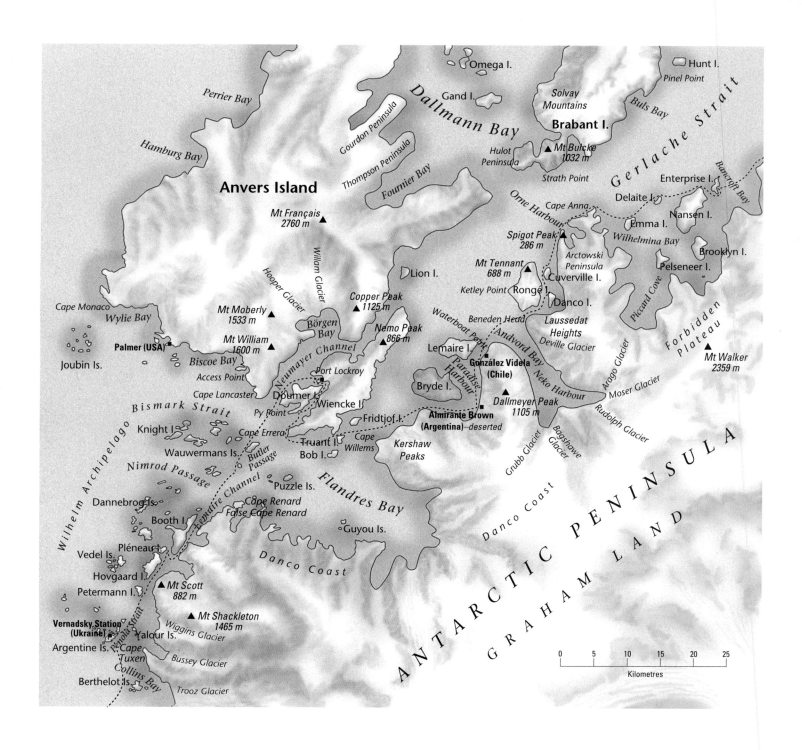

Omega I.

Hunt I.

Pinel Point

Perrier Bay

Gand I.

Dallmann Bay

Solvay Mountains

Brabant I.

Buls Bay

Gerlache Strait

Gourdon Peninsula

Hamburg Bay

Thompson Peninsula

Fournier Bay

Hulot Peninsula

▲ Mt Bulcke 1032 m

Strath Point

Enterprise I.

Bancroft Bay

Delaite I.

Anvers Island

Cape Anna

Nansen I.

Emma I.

Mt Français 2760 m ▲

Orne Harbour

Spigot Peak ▲ 286 m

Wilhelmina Bay

Brooklyn I.

Lion I.

Mt Tennant 688 m ▲

Arctowski Peninsula

Pelseneer I.

William Glacier

Copper Peak 1125 m ▲

Cuverville I.

Hooper Glacier

Ketley Point

Ronge I.

Danco I.

Piccard Cove

Cape Monaco

Mt Moberly 1533 m ▲

Börgen Bay

Nemo Peak 866 m ▲

Lraussedat Heights

Forbidden Plateau

Wylie Bay

Waterboat Point

Beneden Head

Andvord Bay

Arago Glacier

Mt Walker 2359 m

Palmer (USA) ■

Mt William 1600 m ▲

Neumayer Channel

Lemaire I.

Deville Glacier

Joubin Is.

Biscoe Bay

González Videla (Chile) ■

Neko Harbour

Moser Glacier

Access Point

Port Lockroy

Bryde I.

Paradise Harbour

Dallmeyer Peak 1105 m ▲

Rudolph Glacier

Cape Lancaster

Doumer I.

Wiencke I.

Bismark Strait

Py Point

Fridtjof I.

Almirante Brown (Argentina) –deserted

Knight I.

Cape Errera

Truant I.

Cape Willems

Kershaw Peaks

Grubb Glacier

Bagshawe Glacier

Wauwermans Is.

Butler Passage

Bob I.

Nimrod Passage

Lemaire Channel

Puzzle Is.

Flandres Bay

Danco Coast

ANTARCTIC PENINSULA

Dannebrog Is.

Cape Renard
False Cape Renard

Guyou Is.

Danco Coast

Booth I.

Vedel Is.

Pléneau I.

Hovgaard I.

▲ Mt Scott 882 m

Danco Coast

GRAHAM LAND

Petermann I.

Wiggins Glacier

▲ Mt Shackleton 1465 m

Vernadsky Station (Ukraine) ■

Penola Strait

Yalour Is.

Argentine Is.

Cape Tuxen

Collins Bay

Bussey Glacier

Berthelot Is.

Trooz Glacier

0 5 10 15 20 25

Kilometres

Enterprise to Vernadsky

Graham Charles

Yesterday had been spectacular. Today, a blanket of cloud lay low over a choppy sea. As I paddled, my imagination skipped back 85 years to 1916 when, in a sheltered little bay on Enterprise Island, 10 kilometres from Portal Point, the whaling ship *Gouvenoren* caught fire and was run aground. The exposed wreck is now home to nesting Antarctic terns, a popular anchorage for yachts and an attraction for Zodiacs from tour boats. Intrigued by the wreck as we headed into Gouvenoren Harbour, I peered into the gloom. A vague shape began to appear. 'How bizarre!' I thought, staring hard through the snow and mist. There was no doubt that the wreck still had a full mast, rigging and stays. Zooming in with the video as Marcus and Jonesy disappeared behind the hulk, I remained confused until I rounded the bow to find the rigging belonged to the yacht *Sarah J. Verkoork*. Skipper Henk Boersma and the crew were all out on deck to welcome us with steaming mugs of coffee.

I had met Henk and the *Sarah J.* in Ushuaia and it was good to see them again. Steam rose out of our damp clothing as we were invited into the enveloping warmth of the cabin of the first vessel we had seen since Hope Bay. Eight eager pairs of eyes twinkled at us over coffee cups as if they had just found some long-lost Antarctic explorers. The fresh hot coffee was exquisite and our stories were well received.

Enterprise Island was a benchmark in our journey. After 12 days and 500 kilometres of isolated paddling, exposed to the whim and violence of the Drake Passage, we had made it to the shelter of the Palmer Archipelago, the zone known affectionately as the 'banana belt'. Conditions there are often calmer and warmer, with a multitude of offshore islands providing shelter from ocean swells, and plenty of easy beaches for landings and camping. Human presence has a long history in this part of the Peninsula, from the days of whalers and sealers to the scientific bases and stations now scattered along the coast and islands. It is also a popular area for tour and charter boats, so we expected far more human contact for the next few days. From a scratchy radio transmission a week or so before, we knew the *Tooluka* was scheduled to stop soon at Enterprise Island en route to Cuverville Island. It was a great opportunity to talk to some

Old tide marks on an iceberg hint at their instability – their tendency to roll without warning makes them a serious hazard for sea kayakers.

other people and off load 40 or so rolls of shot film and spent video batteries.

Our time on the *Sarah J.* passed all too quickly, and Henk needed to get moving. Reluctantly we began pulling on our clammy jackets when Roger Wallis's unmistakable Aussie twang crackled across Henk's radio. The *Tooluka* was standing off ready to come alongside. I could smell the fresh bread cooking before we even stepped aboard. Like true opportunists we settled into our next story-telling session without missing a beat. Our hosts politely tolerated the wet penguin stench that followed us into the overcrowded cabin. The evening hours were whiled away with a hearty roast dinner and adventure tales. The *Tooluka* crew were in good spirits after skiing and adventures of their own. The snow fell on the deck with a soft patter, and periodic bursts of laughter filtered into the silent Antarctic evening.

The *Sarah J. Verkoork* at Enterprise Island.

It was after midnight when Roger dropped us at the campsite we'd carved out of snow earlier in the day, dodging the feisty little dive-bombing terns. As we hurried to crawl into damp sleeping bags while still warmed by the heat of the *Tooluka* cabin, snow fell on the tent with the same consistency as the gloopy porridge we ate for breakfast each morning.

Even when you're living a dream come true, there are days that suck. It happens sometimes, even when you are totally accustomed to your workload and position. From the moment we waved goodbye to the *Tooluka* through the snow and mist, I couldn't get comfortable. Everything felt heavy. I was cold. My boat had an imaginary lean that no amount of trimming could fix. The thermos in the cockpit dug into my leg. Even the water seemed wetter.

Now that we were in the 'banana belt' I wanted to slow up a little, paddle between the islands and see the countryside. The idea was purely academic, however, as the snow increased and the wind picked up. We tucked into our hoods and disappeared into our own worlds, following a compass bearing through the misty, snow-blown world.

A rocky point loomed like a road sign in the mist. Jonesy popped his head out of his jacket like a tortoise. He readjusted the compass, grunted something we couldn't hear over the wind, slipped back into his hood and led the way into the murk, heading for the invisible western tip of Emma Island some six kilometres away.

This was a game of 'join the dots' Antarctic style and for me was the least pleasing part of the trip.

Although it was important we paddled as a group, the days were often long solitary affairs, buried deep in our jackets alone with our personal thoughts.

Marcus loves to paddle in straight lines. He revels in the opportunity to paddle without distraction, uninterrupted by scenery or shooting photos. He is inspired by the technical action of swinging his blades. I tailed him and Jonesy in a mood as black as the weather. My butt was killing me. My shoulders screamed. I had long since given up on the day. This was one of those times when I was supposed to take pleasure in my pain, push through the threshold, endure and all sorts of other expeditionary clichés. None of them worked – I was bored and I hurt. Minutes seemed like hours, but nothing happens in minutes in Antarctica.

The evidence of our physical passing along this frozen coast existed only briefly, sketched in the water by the dip of the paddle and the slice of the keel, and then it was gone. The spiritual trail was etched permanently in my soul by hard work, challenging elements and anxiety about the unknown. Emma Island loomed out of the mist and disappeared again. There was no landing on these islands protected by crumbling ice cliffs and black craggy capes. The bitter northeasterly harried us as we approached Cape

Anna off the Arctowski Peninsula.

A heavy blanket of cloud clung to everything like plastic lunch wrap. I knew that a beautiful rock spire, known as the Zeiss Needle, lay just beyond Spigot Point and up in the clouds. I'd seen pictures of it in books and didn't want to miss seeing it for real. Heedless of my desire, the clouds clung and the drizzle drizzled. Anger and impatience are always useless emotions in the natural world, and Antarctica pulled no punches in reminding me of this.

It was getting late in this dismal day and we'd been looking in vain for a campsite. Marcus had disappeared in the distance, heading for Cuverville Island where we knew there was a popular landing spot. I was trailing miserably, shooting a few photographs. Despite my poor vision, I'm a very visual person. Most of all, I love the rare occasions when I trip the camera shutter and know in that split second I have captured some magic ingredient that expresses exactly what I feel or want to say. Ahead of me, Jonesy turned to look over his shoulder for me. He looked bone tired, but still concerned about where I was. That split second in time when Jonesy locked his tired eyes on mine remains as clear in my mind as the photo I took.

Marcus and Jonesy arrived at Cuverville 20 minutes ahead of me. We had planned to paddle 20 kilo-metres, but twice that distance had slid by the hulls in eight and a half hours. My mood followed a rapid barometric rise, lifting with the cloud, brightening with rays of sunshine and finally a great view of the Zeiss Needle guarding the Errera Channel like a stone gatekeeper. Towering walls of clean stone, steep enough to shrug off the most persistent ice from the Gerlache Strait tempests, rose from an apron of ice and snow. Higher still, the vertical walls gave way to a craggy summit capped with impossibly balanced mushrooms of ice. Night crept in. A cup of tea, an easy tent pitch among thousands of gentoos and associated guano, my black mood was gone and everything returned to normal as we settled into sleep.

On a clear, calm day Antarctica is like a vast presence resting without moving a muscle. The trials of the previous day were easily forgotten, and we basked in our first real chance to 'hurry up and do nothing'. We draped every available rock with wet gear. At nearly 7° Celsius, it was hot – hot enough for a wash. Naked bathing in Antarctica will never take off as a major sport. The water is just below 0° Celsius. Exposed skin hurts after 15 seconds. Mountainous gooseflesh erupts in a feeble attempt to halt cooling. Ice cream headache turns into ice cream body-ache. Genital shrinkage is dramatic and alarming. Testicles disappear totally in order to preserve their ability to add to the gene pool at a later, warmer date. Howls and hyperventilation echoed in the still air. The grounded bergs seemed to rock with mirth at our antics. Two hard weeks of sweat, penguin guano, seal excreta and dampness tell an odorous tale, and the feel and smell of fresh air on freshly scrubbed bodies was divine. We laid our foam mats in the sun on rocks overlooking our bay, brewed a coffee, grabbed our books, mirror shades and sun hats and settled in butt naked, Club Med style.

When passengers on a tour vessel depart their ship, safety regulations demand full extreme weather clothing, regardless of the conditions. On a day like this was, they must have been baking and complaining. It can't have helped matters for the tour guides from the 500-berth Antarctic cruise ship *Marco Polo* to round the point into our bay and find three naked campers lolling around on the beach. For four or five hours, the Zodiacs from the vessel kept buzzing into our bay like bees. We'd been expecting to come into contact with people on this part of the Peninsula, but that didn't ease the feeling of invasion. It was difficult, I thought, to find a place on the globe out of range of people in some form of modern transport. As the world's population increases, the amount of space we each have is reduced. Manhattan Island in

An easy landing, great camping and improving weather – time for a wash at Cuverville Island.

New York has nearly 26,000 people per square kilometre. Here I was struggling with 500 extra human beings in 26,000 square kilometres.

The ship left before sunset and our solitude, more imagined than real, returned. We cooked dinner on the rocks as the sun set. The Antarctic landscape was exquisite for photography. The depth and quality of the whites and blues in the sky, ice and snow were offset by unbelievable changing shades of red, pink and blue during the hour-long sunsets. The bergs, like chameleons, reflected the sky. Brabant Island, some 40 kilometres across the Gerlache Strait, was razor sharp in clarity. The bergs glowed and faded in the dying light. Penguins appeared unheralded on the shore, fat from their visits to a krill ground. Night was two hours of semi-darkness as the sun dipped behind the peaks of Rongé Island and the Danco Coast.

The brief business of swimming in Antarctica.

Everyday rituals reveal a lot about the character of your companions on an expedition like this. At bedtime, Jonesy invariably crawled onto his mat wherever it lay, bunching all his spare clothes and gear into a heap. He would work on his collection of crossword puzzles laminated to the back of the charts before going to sleep. Marcus would check that everything was lying just right, his pillow was made up correctly and everything was in order. He would then read for a certain time, pull a shade over his eyes and drift off. I would load a tape into my Walkman and snuggle deep into my bag with the hood done up and drift away to other locations and plans for the future. More often than not, I'd wake in the middle of the night with a sore ear from lying on my headphones.

Our ritual about where to have lunch and a hot drink was another personality metaphor. Whatever the weather or landing possibilities, Marcus would always look ahead, saying 'just one more bay', chasing rainbows for a lunch spot. Jonesy would eat or drink regardless of where he was. I was somewhere in between. It amazed me sometimes that we ended up together, all drinking hot Milo and munching from our lunch bags.

And then there was the morning porridge ceremony. Marcus, on the occasions when he did in fact cook breakfast instead of hiding under his airline eye-shade and pretending the day hadn't started, measured the ingredients at least twice for extra accuracy, following the instructions on the packet to the letter. He would then sit over the pot with his watch running and take it off the stove at the allotted time,

The Errera Channel in calm conditions with the Zeiss Needle behind.

ready or not. Jonesy would throw in anything within reach, even if it wasn't porridge, and do odd jobs while the porridge burned. I would forget where I was up to in the porridge-making process and start another two jobs, eventually trying to recall which I'd started first and what I should do next. Between us, however, we always managed to produce a hot billy of porridge to fuel us for the challenge of the day, be it a storm or a silent cruise on mirror-like water as we continued south.

The area between Cuverville and Rongé islands was once a favoured whaling harbour, and a century ago there would have been half a dozen whalers sheltered there to process their kill. Now, our solitary progress was interrupted only by the snorts of two large leopard seals, poking their large dinosaur heads out of the water. Like curious but very large spotty dogs with canines as long as fingers, they followed us. Apparently deciding they preferred the orange hull of Marcus's boat over the yellow of mine and Jonesy's, both vast animals began snorting around his rudder. 'Get these things off me,' Marcus wailed plaintively as he paddled furiously around in a big circle trying to come back past us and ditch his unwanted escorts. Leopard seals have a reputation for a 'bite first, ask questions later' approach to life. Jonesy's and my hysterical laughter did nothing to help Marcus whose new friends were really warming up to the fun game and harrying him closer and closer. All good things get tiring, however, and eventually they decided that better sport existed elsewhere, disappearing beneath the boat, much to Marcus's relief.

We lunched on Danco Island at an old British base hut abandoned in 1959 after a short life of only three years. The island was named after Emile Danco, a scientist who died on the journey home from the Peninsula.

A breeze was building out of Andvord Bay as we eyed the six-kilometre crossing to Duthier Point. In no time it was blowing a steady 30 knots – a sort of baby katabatic, which we named a 'kitabatic'. Like a river of wind, it swept in front of us while 200 metres behind us the water remained completely calm. We pulled into the lee of a berg and donned full storm gear for the crossing, anxiously gambling that the wind would stay moderate. In the distance, big bergs scattered across the channel. Bashing into the wind and waves, we headed for the shelter of a large, wallowing iceberg. In the relative calm behind it, we hatched more plans, picked our next berg, pulled up hoods and zippers and peeled out into the wind for the next 20-minute thrash.

The moment we got to the lee of Duthier Point and the entrance to Aguirre Passage it was calm again: we had crossed the wind river. Behind us whitecaps were still flowing out the bay. In front of us, just visible in the distance, were the 'Antarctic orange' huts of the Chilean naval base called Presidente Gonzalez Videla on a site known as Waterboat Point. It was the site of one of the more bizarre, and certainly smallest, overwinter expeditions in Antarctic history. Here, in 1921–22 a couple of Brits, 19-year-old Thomas Bagshawe and his almost-as-youthful colleague Maxime Charles Lester, wintered underneath a beached whaling dory in the interests of science. They had a miserable time: their ink froze, their matches didn't work, their accommodation was only a metre high, and they survived on seal and penguin meat. But they did complete the first in-depth account of penguin breeding biology.

Like a cat with a mouse, leopard seals would kill penguins and then present us with the remains.

A penguin colony on Cuverville Island is silhouetted in front of the Zeiss Needle.

In a scene we were becoming accustomed to, the base staff turned out to welcome us, examine our kayaks and ask questions. When we told them we'd left from Hope Bay a couple of weeks ago, the response was typically disbelieving: stupido, loco, crazy! Then they asked which tour boat or yacht we had *really* come from, and where it was anchored.

Our introductions were interrupted by a big leopard seal picking a gruesome fight-to-the-death with the stern of one of the base's Zodiacs. The seal had the hapless craft in its massive jaws. The Zodiac vainly blew air in the seal's face as its teeth tore into the rear pontoon. Alas, it was a one-sided battle, until the Chilean armada came to the rescue and drove the beast off with rocks. They hauled the limp Zodiac to the beach and inspected the wounds. The damage was declared serious, but not fatal and the patient was carried off for surgery. For some reason, leopard seals like the tail ends of Zodiacs: there were 20 or so reported deflations during the summer season.

There are few landings in Paradise Harbour so we happily accepted the offer of a pot-luck dinner, our hosts politely eating our dehydrated food while we munched happily on fresh bread and butter washed down with good Chilean red wine, before tumbling into bed.

We had no fixed plan, no time pressure and no need to be anywhere in particular as we floated off into a calm, grey morning. This was the tao of sea kayaking: to do nothing but not get nothing done. After two hard weeks in this land, we were as at home with it and ourselves as I could imagine. It would have been difficult to find three more contented beings on the planet, and I couldn't think of a place more worthy of our attention. I let Marcus and Jonesy disappear ahead. I loaded a favourite tape into my Walkman and followed along, alone, grinning stupidly and on the verge of tears of happiness.

Pictures in books couldn't possibly do justice to the beauty of Paradise Harbour.

Mountains dropped steeply into the sea, protecting it jealously from wind and weather. The ice cliffs and seracs shifted and cracked in the morning chill. Icebergs, like wild sculptures born of a demented artist's soaring imagination, were embedded in the smooth sea surface. Amid this lunatic art exhibition, any trace of our passing was soon lost.

We ate lunch like school boys sitting together with our legs swinging on the old jetty of the burned and abandoned Argentinian station Almirante Brown. The stillness was complete. It seemed as if the Peninsula was in the same mood as we were – relaxed and happy not to do much. We crashed along in thickening brash, clowning around on weirdly shaped bergs, and setting up silly photographs. A minke whale dropped by briefly. The stillness was absolute: we were in a vacuum of movement.

In front of us sat the Gerlache Strait, the main wind highway separating the Palmer Archipelago from

the mainland. It was late, 5pm, and it seemed a big ask to begin a five-hour crossing at this late hour. Yet to get a windless crossing seemed almost inconceivable, the height of good fortune. Marcus, forever keen to paddle straight and hard, was champing at the bit. We rolled the dice and pushed the Bears into the inky stillness.

We were rewarded. Not a ripple stirred the water save the infinitely spreading v-shaped bow waves. Before midnight another 35 kilometres had passed and we were tiring. The Gerlache had allowed us an unimaginable crossing, and light snow was falling as we robotically set up camp on a rocky northwest point on Truant Island.

Continuing west in the morning we travelled along the eastern side of Wiencke Island beneath the towering Fief Range. We rounded Cape Errera and for the first time since leaving Hope Bay turned north. Like a thin corridor sliced through the mountains, the Peltier Channel creates a narrow waterway between Wiencke and Dourmer islands. We paddled its 11-kilometre length into a tidal outflow and arrived at Port Lockroy in the middle of the afternoon.

The name Port Lockroy conjured up images in my mind of a thriving port in an idyllic location, with wharves, jetties and yachts moored in the bay. Little did we know it was no more than a small rocky islet,

100 metres long and 50 metres wide with couple of small huts, two Brits and what seemed like a couple of million excreting baby gentoo penguins.

The port was used by the whalers in the early 1900s, and bones still litter the beaches there, testimony to man's past actions. Port Lockroy was named in 1904 by French explorer Dr Jean-Baptiste Charcot. During the Second World War, the Peninsula's first dedicated science base was built there as part of the British Naval Operation Tabarin. It was used sporadically until 1962, but it has since been declared an historic site and restored as a museum.

Each summer, a couple of hardy staff members spend three months on the tiny islet with no power or running water. They serve about two ship visits per day, monitor use of the museum, process mail and ensure tourists understand the rules when dealing with the rightful owners – the penguins. We tested the mail service. Our postcards went by ship to the Falkland Islands, then to Britain and then back to New Zealand. We beat our postcards back to New Zealand by at least a month.

We were like celebrity museum artifacts for the next ship that pulled into Port Lockroy, answering endless questions about what we ate, how we went to the toilet and even how did we get there with the kayaks! The pay-off was an invitation to a barbecue aboard the *Kapitan Dranitsyn*. On the ship the questions kept coming, everyone interested in our experience of Antarctica and keen to share their own experiences. Going to Antarctica is like joining a club. It unites people. If you've been there, are there or have even just dreamt of being there, you're touched by its beauty, power, isolation, bare-bones innocence and indifference to life and death. Antarctica generates a potent energy among its followers, and inspires people of all genders, races and creeds to

We would take rest breaks wherever we could get out of the kayaks. Comfort was not a determining factor.

protect it fiercely.

After midnight we curled up on the post office floor and drifted off to sleep with a few thousand postcards from the 'bottom of the world' to all other nations teetering above us on the stamping desk.

With bellies bulging from the previous evening's gorging, we said 'See ya later, mate' to Jim and Ken, the post office men, and arranged radio schedules so Jim could relay news from us to the *Tooluka* when it showed up. The somewhat vague weather information – general wind expected from general directions and the possibility of snow – fell within the limits of kayaking 'tolerance'. At least there were no gale warnings, but Marcus and I canned Jonesy's idea to paddle a further 40 kilometres west to the American Palmer Station on Anvers Island to see elephant seals, and took a bearing for the Wauwerman Islands.

It was a day of joining very small dots as we wove 35 kilometres through the many little rock islets of the Wauwermans along the edge of the Butler Passage to the Lemaire Channel. It was a stretch of water worthy of respect. I'd read a harrowing account of the vessel *Ice Bird* which nearly ran aground in a gale in the islands, struggling with the wind as it tried to reach the Lemaire Channel. On our return journey on board the *Explorer* we encountered winds gusting to 75 knots through the Butler Passage. These surely would have killed us if they'd blown up while we were out there in our kayaks.

Exhausted and relieved, we finally drew directly west of Cape Renard, staring through the cleavage of the two impressive rock spires known as the Amazon's Breasts. Vertical walls abounded along this section of coast and the climbing opportunities looked

Jonesy and Marcus revel in superb conditions through the Lemaire Channel.

Perfect conditions in the Lemaire Channel.

fantastic. We touched land just inside the Lemaire Channel on a beach made up of big round granite boulders. It was a sheltered spot and within a few minutes we were all fast asleep, despite the uncompromising rocks. We awoke an hour later and spurred our tired bodies back into action. The camping wasn't great and the breeze we'd been concerned about earlier had died, leaving the Lemaire Channel mirror calm.

The channel separates Booth Island from the mainland, and its dramatic scenery makes it a major attraction for Antarctic cruise ships. Shaped like an hourglass, at its narrowest point the channel is no more than a kilometre wide. The massive ice cliffs hanging over it from near the top of 1000-metre Wandel Peak periodically avalanche and send tonnes of icy rubble cascading into the water, the debris sometimes bouncing right across the channel. Even the tour ships don't halt for long in the neck of the Lemaire. In our sea kayaks, we were more than a little anxious. Even at our fastest pace, we would be exposed to the danger of avalanching ice for some time. Although we hugged the eastern side, as far away as possible from potential ice falls, the cliffs looming above us looked as though they'd still land on us if a major fall occurred.

One of those rare, magic images sealed itself in my mind with the click of my camera shutter as we neared the end of the Lemaire Channel. Marcus and Jonesy were paddling among a maze of ice blocks in calm water. It wasn't just the beautiful light and good timing, but also some indefinable extra ingredient which told me the whole was going to be greater than the sum of the parts. It was a day I'll never forget: I could have paddled forever. No one spoke. We rounded the southern tip of Booth Island and spied a good beach on nearby Pléneau Island, breaking the 40-kilometre mark again as we touched down for a trouble-

Gentoo chicks were fascinated with our equipment and would spend all night clambering (and pooping) all over it.

Gentoo penguins on
Petermann Island.

free landing in the early evening.

With spectacular views of the towering cliffs of Booth Island and the imposing Mount Scott on the eastern side of the Lemaire Channel, Pléneau is a small granite island, almost ice-free, and is often the southernmost landing point for tour ships. We pitched our tent with the real estate tenet of 'location, location, location' in mind and settled back to enjoy more of our southern paradise.

We had decided that we needed to slow down a little. At our present rate we were going to make the Antarctic Circle very soon and were not sure if the *Tooluka* could get that far south to pick us up. We knew it was going to be delayed by the rescue of the Australian team, but with no radio contact for some time, we didn't know for how long. So we passed the morning catching up on diaries, repairs and other chores.

Enjoying the peaceful conditions, I had been for a walk and was circling the camp looking for a photograph when I heard loud flatulence from near the tent. Weeks of dehydrated food can have this effect, but this was particularly impressive. The first rumbling was joined by a chorus of burps, snorts and more resounding wind. I became concerned for my partners' gastric well-being – not to mention my equipment! A quick investigation revealed that the tent and my gear were safe. The culprits were not my companions, but some newly arrived elephant seals hauled out in a wallow just beyond the tent. This also explained the incredible stench now filling the air. Pléneau is about the southern limit of elephant seals in this sector of Antarctica. Like huge, very huge, fat slugs they lie together during their moult to reduce heat loss. The symphony of bodily functions is extraordinary as they trade burps, farts, roars and snorts in a disgusting, but contented wallow of saltwater and excreta. Jonesy was delighted to see them, after his disappointment at not visiting the Palmer colony.

In a feeble emulation of our slothful role models, we lazed around for the morning. It was a beautiful day but we needed some exercise. Ten kilometres along Penola Strait lay Petermann Island, first charted in 1873 during the Dallmann expedition: their mooring points can still be found on the rocky points either side of the harbour. An Argentinian refugio was built there in 1955 and is now left as an emergency hut with stocks of food, fuel and bedding. When the need for exercise drove us to our boats, it was only two hours of easy cruising before we caught sight of the old refugio in a small bay. With no brash ice to melt for drinking water, we had to wrangle two mini-icebergs from the channel. Young penguins were thick on the ground. We pulled our kayaks up by the hut and sealed all hatches, thankful for the small perimeter fence around the porch and door of the refugio. It put us just clear of their puckered anuses and projectile range of about 1.5 metres.

We found the hospitality at all the international bases fantastic, and the Ukrainians at Vernadsky Station in the Argentine Islands were no exception.

Penguins, especially the young ones, are delightful. Refreshingly unafraid and curious, even a baby will stand its ground in front of you until it has to peer so far up it topples backwards. In no time, chicks were checking out every nook and cranny of our kayaks. Eventually one achieved the stunning feat of jumping its own height onto the edge of the deck. Its little penguin feet blurred like a cartoon character as it scrabbled for traction on the slippery gel coat surface. Finally it hooked a piece of deck cord and stood up proudly. Like a newly crowned king it announced its arrival with a 'squark', much waving of its downy fins and a quality projectile excreta across the deck. The others tried the jump but the new king proceeded to head butt any who tried to share his kingdom. They toppled, landed flat on their backs and were unceremoniously shunted out of the way so another could have a shot. Soon the new king tired and retreated for a sleep to the neoprene spraydeck which must have felt incredibly soft after life on the cold stony ground.

Great opportunities come to all, but many don't know they have met them. The only preparation to take advantage of them is simple fidelity to what each day brings.

A E Dunning

If penguins are the personalities of the Antarctic wildlife community, then the Ukrainians are the characters of human culture on the Peninsula. Ten kilometres away, tucked in a maze of narrow rock-lined channels on the Argentine Island group, lay the Ukrainian Vernadsky Station. Vernadsky used to be the British base Faraday, built in 1954 for science and sledging expeditions to the south. In 1994 it was sold to the Ukrainian government for the princely sum of £1. Nowadays a team of 16 or so Ukrainians winter over each year, relieved in March by a new crew.

We had heard that the Ukrainians would trade strange concoctions of liquor for items of personal clothing from shipborne tourists. Rumours abounded of the bra and pantie collection behind the bar. We were absolutely sure they weren't going to ask for any of our underwear! Mid-afternoon we picked our way through the island maze, not really planning to stay for long. But once someone caught sight of our kayaks, the whole base turned out to see us, help haul the kayaks out of the water and drag us to the bar. It was only 3pm but Vernadsky was perhaps a fitting place to mark the end of this section of our journey: where humans past and present have carved out a place for themselves among the islands and bays of this relatively sheltered area.

The base doctor, also the barman, produced three sizeable glasses and a plastic bottle of strange amber fluid with things floating in it. We had been warned of the Vernadsky homemade vodka. Now we were confronted with it and had nowhere to run. The glasses were filled to the brim and we were coached in the traditional salutation, 'bud mo na dobranich' (Goodnight my friend, I will see you tomorrow). Once it was perfected, we saluted in unison and downed our medicine. It burned the whole way down. As we began to stumble, they kindly led us to the workout room where we slept among the exercise machines beneath posters of topless Russian beauties. As one of the scientists said, 'I lose many kilograms for this girl!' Outside the Peninsula stretched south ahead of us, uninhabited, waiting while we slept.

I had come to the Peninsula to hear Antarctica speak. I heard the crackle of million-year-old air escaping its icy prison and joining the present day. I heard the unconcerned 'whoosh' of humpback exhalation, and the silence of a land so powerful that even the silence is deafening. I experienced the infinite voices of the Antarctic orchestra wind section: the tenor saxophone katabatic, loud and domineering; the flute-like zephyr moving soft and calm; the bass moaning through ice and rocks. I came to Antarctica to see ice. I saw infinite variations of blue and white, the colour changes so subtle the difference was almost imperceptible. I saw shapes so extraordinary as to be not of this world. I had come to explore a land unknown to me; to make a journey where I listened far more than I spoke. In the simplicity of Antarctica, where the elements are few but powerful, less is definitely more.

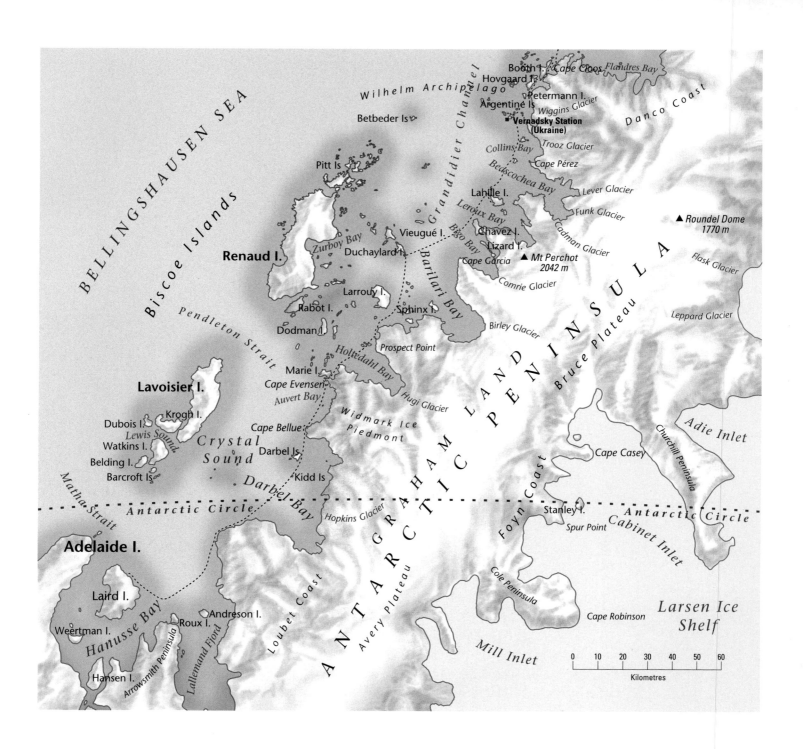

BELLINGSHAUSEN SEA

Booth I. · Cape Cloos · *Flandres Bay*
Hovgaard I.
Wilhelm Archipelago · Petermann I.
Argentine Is · *Wiggins Glacier*
Betbeder Is · *Danco Coast*
■ Vernadsky Station
(Ukraine)
Collins Bay · *Trooz Glacier*
Pitt Is · Cape Pérez
Biscoe Islands · *Bedscochea Bay*
Lahille I. · *Lever Glacier*
Leroux Bay · *Funk Glacier*
Vieugué I. · ▲ Roundel Dome
1770 m
Zurboy Bay · Chavez I.
Renaud I. · Duchaylard I. · Lizard I. · *Cadman Glacier*
Cape García · ▲ Mt Perchot
2042 m
Barilari Bay · *Flask Glacier*
Larrouy I. · *Comrie Glacier*
Rabot I. · Sphinx I.
Dodman I. · *Birley Glacier* · *Leppard Glacier*
Pendleton Strait · Prospect Point
Bruce Plateau
Marie I. · *Holtedahl Bay*
Lavoisier I. · Cape Evensen
Auvert Bay · *Hugi Glacier*
Dubois I. · Krogh I. · *Widmark Ice*
Piedmont · *Adie Inlet*
Lewis Sound
Watkins I. · Cape Bellue
Crystal · Cape Casey
Belding I. · *Sound* · Darbel Is · *Churchill Peninsula*
Barcroft Is · Kidd Is
Darbel Bay
Matha Strait · **Antarctic Circle** · Stanley I. · **Antarctic Circle**
Hopkins Glacier · Spur Point · *Cabinet Inlet*
Adelaide I. · *Foyn Coast*
Cole Peninsula
Laird I. · Andreson I.
Roux I. · *Larsen Ice*
Weertman I. · *Shelf*
Hanusse Bay · Cape Robinson
Loubet Coast
Avery Plateau
Hansen I. · *Arrowsmith Peninsula* · *Lallemand Fiord* · Cape Robinson
Mill Inlet

ANTARCTIC PENINSULA

GRAHAM LAND

0 10 20 30 40 50 60
Kilometres

The Lonely Southern Coast

Mark Jones

'The sea surface has started to freeze in the sheltered bays behind Vernadsky, and I wonder how much further south we can push before we put ourselves in danger of not being picked up by *Tooluka*,' I wrote in my diary the chilly morning we left Vernadsky Station. Overnight the barometer had dropped, and the wind had got up to 50 kilometres an hour, whining like a caged animal. Sleeping inside the base, we were warm and cosy. I should have been thankful that our tent was not being subjected to the gale, but it felt wrong being indoors, just as it did every other time we had stopped at a base. I had a romantic view of Antarctic journeying, the product of reading the stoic accounts of the Heroic Age of exploration, when the continent was uninhabited and travellers had only themselves to rely on. Yet the people who work on the Peninsula these days are an integral part of any coastal experience, and to refuse their hospitality would have been to contrive the journey. But I was damned if could shake the feeling that we were cheating as the wind hammered the base.

South of Vernadsky, there were no more bases: from there on we were on our own and didn't expect to see anybody else for the duration of the journey. We knew the least about this section of coastline. Our maps showed the coast south of Vernadsky carved by deep bays and fiords with few, if any, landings apparent for 200 kilometres. The mountain chains rise sheer from the sea and giant glaciers run between the two. Our plan was to island-hop for the most part to avoid the worst of the katabatic winds that descend from these mountains and sweep out to sea; islands and the odd cape offered the only possibility of landing anyway.

None of us was oblivious to the potential of the weather to stop us in our tracks any time it chose, but we had gained confidence in our decision-making in the Antarctic environment, emboldened by the fact we had come so far with relatively little strife. We had faith in ourselves now, and we knew we could count on each other to deliver. We moved with a certain assurance, even in hostile weather.

At the back of our minds, however, lurked warnings of what we hadn't yet experienced, especially as

To share this land with its creatures was both humbling and a privilege.

the summer drew to a close: the unforgiving savagery of Antarctica. Connecting with our pick-up and achieving all we wanted to was starting to weigh heavily on us. We wondered how much further on we could push before we put ourselves in danger of not being picked up by the *Tooluka*. Roger's last words to us had been, 'Don't get too far south or I won't find you!'

Lahille Island was our first destination. My scribblings from Ushuaia said this was a good place to land. It wasn't. I don't know why this surprised us, for we no longer had much faith in Jerome's hazy recollections which I had diligently noted down all those weeks ago. Lahille Island was like a mountain submerged. All aspects were steep, and we paddled further and further along its precipitous shores in search of the promised landing. We found nothing suitable and kayaked half an hour back to a group of islets we had passed that looked more friendly, frustrated at having paddled an hour for nothing.

The campsite we ended up with was stunning – perched on a snowy knoll with fantastic views of bergs silhouetted against a sky that burnt like a great bonfire for an hour or more. As we watched the show, an enormous iceberg turned over. Great waterfalls of golden water poured off its flanks, and a mighty surge pulsed out in an expanding ring of ice debris. Its above-water shape looked completely different. Our respect for the ice was reinforced once again.

As we journeyed south the scenery became even more dramatic. Each bay was a sweeping vista. Ice cliffs scribed a hard line between land and sea, broken only by glaciers tumbling in vast, broken rivers from peaks that stretched back to the frozen heart of the land.

Our campsites also continued to be dramatic. A day later, we landed on a stony finger of ground barely above the tide on the

Camping on small islands was our only chance of landing during the southern leg of the journey. Cape Evensen at the north end of Auvert Bay.

A big sky at Cape Bellue.

small and otherwise ice-cliffed Duchaylard Island. Snow flurries swirled about us, reducing the bergs grounded in the shallows to ghostly grey shapes. Duchaylard Island was a beggar's choice of a campsite, but 20 kilometres from the mainland you take what you can get. We were thankful to get ashore, despite the matted fur and guano.

Fearful of katabatics, we had paddled solidly that day, an inquisitive young Weddell seal the only diversion. Paddling abreast, we had some good talks on those sorts of days – conversations about life, women, work, women, marriage, women – before drifting apart again to ponder anew.

We awoke at midnight to the wind flogging the tent and got up to beef up the cairns of rocks on the valances. By morning the wind had eased, but odd flying-saucer clouds hovered over the mountains with tidy stacks of lenticular clouds over some of the peaks. An unusual easterly blew. It was hard to read this weather and it looked unstable. Despite this we packed up, not wanting to spend another night so vulnerable to the sea. We were only a metre above the high tide line, and a decent swell or the wash from a collapsing berg would reach that. There was much anxious looking at dropping barometers and the ominous mountains and sky.

'Doggone!' said Graham as we passed Dog Island, thus beginning a half hour of bad puns on place-names down the Peninsula that had us giggling like kids. We found humour in the trivia of our days, in exaggeration of the ridiculous, and in each other. We had gotten to know our idiosyncrasies and took delight in poking fun at our differences.

Bergs like ghostly ships drifted past, and brash ice crackled like battered fish in a frying pan. Ice cliffs thundered in the distance. As the snow flurries grew heavier, I took a compass bearing,

In the simplicity of Antarctica, where the elements are few but powerful, less is definitely more.

and we paddled along in eerie white space. I felt a part of the place by then, and it didn't seem such a wild thing to set our compasses and head blindly for the tiny Tadpole Island through the wall of white, weaving through brash and berg.

At first, the island could have been another iceberg emerging from the gloom, but this one continued to grow, sprouting rocks beneath the ice bluffs. We bore towards the coast. Unseen ice cliffs growled like living things, every so often roaring as they shed a burden of blocks into the heaving sea. Snow plastered our jackets and blanketed the growlers and brash ice. It also formed patches of slush ice, sticky to paddle through.

We were intent on reaching an abandoned refugio marked on our maps at Prospect Point and soon saw it in the distance as a black blob set in the far side of a bay. The prospect of staying in an old hut after such a wet day was enormously appealing, and we marched optimistically towards it. Its windows were boarded up. The interior was black, dank, dripping wet and foetid with mould. Our disappointment was acute but short-lived; we soon saw the humour in the situation, and before long we had dug a flat shelf in the snow and had the tent up.

Diary, 9 February: 'Barometer stable overnight, but now sinking further and incessant rain coming down in sheets since last night. The horizon a dark grey band above the brash ice in our bay, and all the while the ice cliffs at the back of the bay groan and growl and heave great blocks of ice into the tide with a roar. Great to be in our tent, coffee in hand – life is good.'

We had made good progress: an average of 33 kilometres per paddling day and an overall daily average of 25 kilometres since we left Hope Bay. Since we were well ahead of schedule, there was

Whatever you vividly imagine, ardently desire and enthusiastically act upon, must inevitably come to pass.

P Meyer

Our camp at Prospect Point was restful and calm, a chance to savour the remoteness of this southern part of the Peninsula.

less urgency to push south. In fact, we began to deliberately slow our progress.

At Prospect Point we really kicked back and breathed deep of the peace and solitude about us. We stayed for three days, resting, reading, exploring and filming the ice cliffs collapsing. It was an opportunity for our bodies to mend. Graham was on the anti-inflamatories again. My back and I had found a level of discomfort we could both live with.

In this remotest of places, we woke next day to the sound of an outboard motor and, poking our heads from the tent, we found 30 people exploring the bay. Anchored offshore was the *Professor Molchanov*, one of the few vessels that venture so far south. The tour leader was Angus Finney who had sea kayaked a short section of the coast some years ago. He strode up to us with a hand extended, saying, 'Bloody good job, you guys!' Then, in a lighter tone, 'You bastards, I was hoping to do this next year.' We knew of him and he of us. It was nice to meet the man who had first thought to kayak along the coast of the southern-most continent. He of all people understood what an amazing experience it was, and we swapped tales with him for some time. His passengers, though less comprehending, seemed to find us an interesting change from penguins, asking us questions:

'Is that your ship in the bay?'

'No, that's your ship, the *Professor Molchanov.*'

'Oh yes, so it is. So where is your ship, I don't see it in the bay?'

Or:

'Where did your tour leave from and can anybody go on it?'

And:

'Where do you go to at night?'

'We stay in that tent.'

'Yes, but where do you go to after that, to sleep?'

The *Molchanov* left us with some luxuries. We cooked an omelette for lunch and had it on thick slices of Russian bread while beer chilled in the snowmelt creek running past the door of our tent.

They were magical days at Prospect Point: calm evenings, the icebergs lit up like lumps of gold, while the brash ice was drawn from the bay as though a giant hand were pulling on a corner of the ocean. Ice cliffs barked and groaned and shook loose scales of ice, as the last light of day painted the glaciers pink. I tried to capture such scenes with my camera, but it seemed a crude tool for the job, like using a press to preserve the beauty of a flower. Some things are best recorded as impressions on the soul.

It was an ideal opportunity to get some footage of us paddling among the bergage in the bay, and Graham and I did so, while Marcus rolled video from the shore.

We went in search of a leopard seal we had seen earlier on a floe drifting across the bay. Leopard seals are magnificent animals, with heads all out of proportion to their bodies. They have a distinctly reptilian look, as though God used leftover parts when he built them: a giant lizard head attached to the body of a seal. The massive jaws possess a vicious-looking set of teeth. We had read the explorer Frank Worsley's tale of a leopard seal launching from the water and hounding its human victim across the ice. That particular beast was shot and consequently eaten by Ernest Shackleton's men. Worsley observed, 'A man on foot in deep snow, and unarmed would not have a chance…. They attack without provocation, looking on man as a penguin or seal.'

We eventually came across our own beast, sleeping. Graham filmed the 'dramatic encounter' as we drifted closer, expecting the seal to rear up any moment and bare its ivories at us. Never has there been a less enthusiastic villain in a plot, totally uninterested in anything other than remaining in a state of near-coma. I bumped his floe with my kayak, and he half-opened a lazy eye. Television viewers would just have to accept the simple truth that leopard seals don't attack people on sight. The usual extent of their interest is mild curiosity – much to our relief, I might add.

The Butt Naked Canoe Club on tour in Antarctica.

'We're getting pretty crusty,' Marcus announced one day. He wasn't lying. It was close to a month since we'd last washed. We smelt like penguin guano; salt encrusted our jackets and sweat stained our clothes. The bay was the perfect place for a swim to wash away weeks of sweat and grime. It was a short and violent plunge beneath the sea; the water temperature was below zero and in the shade the air was 5° Celsius, but the sun was warm and we emerged gasping and basked like Weddell seals on the rocks to warm up.

'It's one of the great truths of life,' Marcus commented.

'What's that?'

'You never regret a cold swim.'

He was right. Even in Antarctica.

Graham added to his Butt Naked Canoe Club photo collection as we posed nude before the tripod, immortalising one of the lighter moments of the trip.

Relaxing and intensely satisfying, our main pursuit at Prospect Point was capturing collapsing ice cliffs on camera. Lodged on a comfortable seat among the rocks, video camera focused on a huge block poised to topple, sunglasses on, we'd lie back, engrossed in a novel, until a loud crack would have our fingers stabbing for the record button.

One evening a 100-carriage freight train rumbled past our bay. On and on it thundered until I was compelled to poke my head out of the tent. Across the bay a colossal section of glacier had collapsed. The ice debris from it fanned out across the bay in a sweeping line of wreckage, far in excess of our kayaks' top speed, rumbling on and on, diminishing reluctantly like a receding storm. More casual violence played out on a grand scale.

Life was simple. Time rich, we lived in the moment and breathed deep of the untrammelled wildness of the place. Everything made sense there; no waiting at red lights at an empty intersection, no bus-stop faces, blank as blotters, or senses dulled by the stink and din of a city. Our days were ordered by the barometer, the sea and what we could read into our charts; not by signs that began 'Please refrain…'. Life was real, and consequence swift. Ignoring a sign in the city could get you towed; missing a sign in the ice could get you killed.

We had lived with the elements for a while now, and I felt a part of the place. Leopard seals and whiteouts no longer held menace, and I felt as much a part of the coast as the Weddell and the whale. It was a false sense of place. We would always be strangers, existing largely at the whim of the wind and ice and swell.

Rested and revitalised, we set out once more heading south to Marie Island and Cape Evensen. With no landings looking likely for a considerable distance, I wolfed down a couple of our custom-made 'Lard Bars', only to soon pass a small island that offered a campsite. 'We can't stop now,' I said, 'I've just eaten 500 calories!' I pitched the tent, hauled up the boats and grabbed a supply of ice from the tide, feeling

Graham and Jonesy, Prospect Point.

Surf landings were frightening, with freezing water and floating chunks of concrete-hard ice to negotiate.

particularly energetic. And, as at almost every other place we had camped, penguins provided the comic relief: the Charlie Chaplins of the animal world.

In contrast to the comical penguins, the coast was increasingly unforgiving, bounded by ice cliffs, mountains and glaciers. It was a study in the states of water, an ever-changing drama, moving at the patient pace of the ages. The swell wore constantly at the ice. Landings were scarce and sometimes desperate.

At Cape Bellue, the roar of surf on the cape was constant as we searched for a landing. Huge plumes of water blasted skywards behind the headland. Those same waves curled around the cape to break on the granite flank where we were forced to go ashore. Further south the coast was a vast unchecked sweep of ice cliff as far as the eye could see. Behind me, Cape Bellue climbed in rocky steps to the snow; avalanches thundered from ice cliffs that crouched above the bay and grounded bergs listed like wrecked ships, the swells pounding into them now and then to smash off a prow or blast spume from holes in their sides. It was as dramatic a place as I could imagine.

I had made it ashore, picking my moment and running my boat onto the granite before quickly dragging it clear. Brash ice clanked in the waves as I watched Marcus and Graham, yet to make their run. Marcus had edged into shallower water, contemplating the landing, when a big swell reared up behind him, and it was suddenly obvious he was going to get munched.

'Paddle, Marcus! Paddle!' I yelled as the wave broke behind him, the first of a set. With horror movie fascination, I watched as he wrestled with each wave, somehow avoiding being smashed onto the rocks. He escaped to the deeper water with the wallowing bergs. My heart was in my mouth. It was our 30th day on the Peninsula and this would be camp 20, if we could get ashore.

I watched the next wave foam onto the granite teeth of the cove. Marcus chose his moment and ran his kayak up onto a ramp of rock, and we pulled his boat clear. Then Graham went for it, timing his run between swells. Another successful landing, another day closer to the Antarctic Circle.

The line between land and sea is blurred by ice, in which the two find common ground for a distance. It is a zone in constant flux, its heartbeat the glacial thud and shudder, its voice the whip crack of cleaved ice and the skua's cry. It speaks of life and death and the raw beauty of the icescape and promises nothing but endless change and the age-old cycle of freeze and thaw.

I imagined us from afar as specks kayaking against that endless wall of white. The perspective demanded humility. Antarctica wields its power openly and often. The tidal waves, or the bergs that rolled without warning, or those that collapsed into a blocky soup of brash ice, or the contradiction of a berg ploughing into the wind, smashing into swells like a great shapeless barge – all these were indifferent to us and our plans.

We stayed another day at Cape Bellue purely because it was such a stunning place. The scenes we witnessed there will stay with me forever. Marcus and I climbed the escarpment behind the cape to take it all in while Graham gave his chilblains a break. To the north lay Renard Island, looking for all the world like a polar ice cap. In fact we referred to it as the North Pole. To our west, Lavoisier Island looked the same, so it became the West Pole. Bastardising place-names was our way of personalising the places.

From the cape we could look down on Auvert Bay, which we had crossed the day before, and we watched a katabatic in progress. A sinister dark tongue of water, flecked with whitecaps, licked into Crystal Sound: a river of dense wind pouring from the plateau and flowing out across the sea. About this time, unbeknown to Marcus and me, a gale hit our camp and wreaked havoc. Graham did a great job of

With the kayaks getting lighter we were able to make higher average speeds in the latter part of the expedition.

battening down the hatches and nothing of value was lost.

Rain and sleet rattled on the tent next morning. It was a bleak day, the sea steely grey. Scud covered the sea, which had thrown itself at the granite all night. Our humour was still in good form. We had sore stomach muscles from a session of 'paper, scissors, rock' to determine who would get the cream of mushroom soup. Each dinner pack invariably had one soup sachet different from the other two and always more favoured (if only because it was different from the others). We found the situation hilarious, but to an outside observer it would have seemed that we were entering the early stages of madness.

With Marcus behind the camera, and Graham and I as stuntmen, we shot some rough water footage for the documentary, using a reef that lay close to the cape. With each swell, the reef seemed to sink into the sea before the waves rushed back into the void, crashing into one another in a huge foaming haystack. I did half a dozen passes of the breaking reef, heart pounding. The kayak took a big hit from a wave, and I surfed through foaming reflection waves and called time out, worried that my days were numbered in that zone. But the director wanted more, so I managed two more passes before I called it a day. The footage looked great as we reviewed it afterwards, and I decided it was well worth the grey hair.

On the radio to Port Lockroy we heard of six-metre swells in the Drake, perhaps the reason for the *Tooluka*'s delay. We also wondered what effect the rescue of the Australian climbers would have, both on the *Tooluka*'s schedule and on Roger's enthusiasm for adventure. The more we pushed south, the more he would be sticking his neck out to support us.

Should we push for Marguerite Bay or wait for Roger to show? The familiar, consuming debate began again. We were in a difficult position, trying to make a decision without knowing where or what the *Tooluka* was doing. We were obligated to the film crew on board to deliver the five days of filming they required. We also didn't want to force Roger further south than he was happy to go – he had not ventured below the Antarctic Circle before. On the other hand, our personal goal had been to reach Marguerite Bay, and we desperately wanted to achieve that. We knew we could get there; we just didn't know if we could get back again. If only we could have communicated with the *Tooluka* by radio, we could have solved our dilemma, but the vessel remained inexplicably silent. We wasted enormous amounts of energy anguishing, trying to fathom why the *Tooluka* wasn't in radio range of Port Lockroy, which we could still reach with our own HF set on a good night.

Now and then spooky things happen out of the blue which make you realise it is sometimes better to be lucky than good. That evening, after another day's paddling, our tent was pitched on a lonely outcrop of sharp rock on the snow-capped Kidd Islands, which offered the last possibility to camp before the

Antarctic Circle and also broke up the vast crossing of Darbel Bay. But they were not inspiring. We shovelled snow onto shards of stone, secured the tent with plenty of rocks and called it home. We had just turned in for the night when I heard the roar of what I took to be an approaching wind gust. Suddenly the sound was all about us, yet the tent remained still. I looked out the door to see a whitewater torrent,

Graham's birthday card, Antarctic style.

complete with standing waves, hydraulics and haystack waves, rushing between our islet and the next. It was met by a pulse of water surging round the other side of our rock. We could only guess that a major glacial collapse had taken place some distance away on the coast. Had we been on Duchaylard Island such a wave would have wiped all trace of us into the freezing sea.

By now the Antarctic Circle, circumscribing the globe at 66° 33' South, was just an hour or so south, tantalisingly close. The problem of meeting up with the *Tooluka* consumed us. Roger had expected to be in the area on 15 February. It was now the 18th and he wasn't even in radio contact.

We discussed our situation.

'In two days we'll be out of food,' Marcus reminded us. 'If *Tooluka* was within two days of us we would have radio contact by now.'

'Going further south means we'll almost certainly lose contact with Port Lockroy,' cautioned Graham. 'From where we are, on a good night we can just get a message through to them.'

We decided to stay put until we heard from the *Tooluka*.

It was Graham's birthday. Marcus and I wrote 'Happy Birthday Grum' (his nickname) in brash ice on the beach and told him what a good bastard we thought he was for being born. We decided to celebrate by paddling across the Antarctic Circle, only five kilometres away. So we set off with the GPS to find the elusive line we had come so far to cross. Marcus kept an eye on the GPS, and after almost an hour he called a halt. Together we coasted over latitude 66° 33' South. We had saved a tot of Cutty Sark whisky for the occasion, and we sat in our boats, warmed our bellies and slapped each other on the back. We had done what no one else had tried and felt pretty darn good about it. It's not every day you can claim a world first.

To save fuel on melting brash ice, we had got into the habit of collecting cooking and drinking water from puddles of melt-water and drips from the icicles that fringed the snowpack. That evening I ruined the dinner and our three coffees using that trick. The tidal wave the night before had washed a lot higher than I realised and saturated the snowpack with salt. We were running low on dinners so I strained the sauce out of our curry to make it edible. 'Dinner's up, team. Beef and bean soup tonight…'

We were contemplating sleep when the radio crackled into life. '*Explorer, Expl…. Yormolova…*' We tuned in to the broken conversation between the two vessels. The upshot was that, 150 kilometres south of us, a vessel called *Explorer* was planning to steam as far south as Adelaide Island, then head back north late the following day. Graham's genius for scenting a scam came to the fore. 'What if we were to meet up with them and hitch a ride north?' he mused. It would solve our dilemma created by the *Tooluka*'s silence, but it meant the end to our dreams of reaching Marguerite Bay.

Graham picked up the radio: '*Explorer, Explorer,* Kiwi Kayakers. How copy?' We stared at the radio, willing it to answer. The static crackled and spat like brash ice in a billy. We leant closer. A voice leapt from the radio, 'Kiwi Kayakers, Kiwi Kayakers. This is Kim. Copy you 5 out of 10, over.' Five minutes later a ride north had been offered if we wanted it. The catch was we were 90 kilometres away from where they could pick us up at Hannuse Bay on Adelaide Island.

We reach the Antarctic Circle, 66° 33' S.

We had no time to spare. As well as the distance to be overcome, Lallemand Fjord lay to the south of us. On our map it looked like a sleeping dragon, gaping at the sea, as though a giant fist had punched a hole into the very lungs of the land. It was a perfect drain for those vast expanses of cold heavy air. The *Antarctic Pilot* warned of its katabatics.

We needed to paddle through the night if we were to make the rendezvous with *Explorer*. Haste and excitement took hold, tinged with apprehension. We knew we were setting ourselves up for an epic paddling leg. It was 10.15pm as we left. The sky was on fire with colour, and bergs were silhouetted against the horizon like spilt chess pieces. It felt great to be finally heading south with some urgency.

We didn't stop at the Antarctic Circle this time. It lay in the middle of Darbel Bay far from anywhere, and we bent our backs toward the darkening horizon. Graham is night blind: he becomes sightless as the light fades into twilight.

'Jonesy, Marcus, I've lost you.'

'Over here, go hard left.'

'What?'

By the end of the journey, the twilight was lengthening as the Polar night stretched out to five-and-a-half hours.

'*Hard* left!'

Kathunk! 'Damn.'

'That's a growler. Over this way.'

Beneath old blue stars and a sickle moon, we continued in this fashion, trying to second-guess the brash field. The water winked with phosphorescence, little flashes of light different from anything I had seen before.

As light seeped back into the world, we heard gunshots and the distant rumble of artillery. The glaciers were waking up.

It was like kayaking in a freezer. Ice built up on the kayaks with each splash as we wove through a maze of bergs and ploughed through syrup-like patches of semi-frozen sea. Our boats were heavy with ice glaze, the deck compass a frozen blob. Only our arms, always moving, avoided the armour coating. The further south we pushed, the denser the icefield became. Ahead a jumble of bergs hunched shoulder to shoulder. We had run out of leads in an icefield that seemed to have no end. There was nothing for it but to backtrack and head out to sea.

We had arranged a radio schedule with *Explorer* at 5am. On the Matsuyama Rocks, we landed on a rock shelf between swells. In the time it took to call in our position and wolf down a half ration pack for breakfast, our toes and fingers became useless with cold. We made a hurried departure.

Lallemand Fjord's great maw reached back into the mountains, breathing easy for now, and we pointed our bows to the farther shore. The hours passed. The dragon dozed. We had not quite reached the safety of the far shore when the breeze became wind, the wind increased to a gale, and the tops were whipped away from the steepening waves. With the ice cliffs of Laird Island approaching off our beam, we abandoned our objective and gave the wind our backs. We surfed the waves to the shelter of bergs

Paddling through the night was a surreal experience, with all water drips freezing instantly on the decks of our kayaks – our thoughts were with Shackleton.

The end of the journey – the crew of the *Explorer* help us with our packs.

and eventually to a cove we could land in. It had been 16 hours of hard graft. We lay like three Weddells while the billy boiled.

Three hours later Graham made VHF radio contact with *Explorer*. The katabatic had blown itself out, and we had one more hour's paddling to go. Our kayaking expedition was almost over.

Sometimes there is a moment where nothing is spoken but everything is said. As we sat in our kayaks for what would be the last time, a baby minke whale arrived with a sigh. It slid between our kayaks, ever so slowly, close enough to touch, then drifted beneath us upside down, the green-white of its belly centimetres below our boats. Finally, spy-hopping from the water, it fixed us with a glistening eye before vanishing beneath the brash. It was a touching farewell from the Peninsula we had come to feel a part of and to love so much: it was difficult to say goodbye. But pancake ice was already beginning to form on the sea in places. Winter was fast approaching. It was time for us to go.

In the deep waters of Hannuse Bay, the *Explorer* waited. A bottle of champagne had been put up by the captain for the first passenger to sight us, and the rails were lined with red-jacketed hopefuls. Our boats were hoisted aboard, and salt-encrusted and bearded, we took the gangplank, to enter a separate reality of water on tap, showers on call, five-course meals and people who didn't smell like penguins. It was an unreal experience to be plucked from the wildness of one reality and dropped into the luxury and security of another, but we adapted quickly. The passengers were under the impression that we had been rescued, and we became a novelty on board. In exchange for the lift north, we gave a presentation about our trip and the philosophy of adventure we shared. We steamed through a full gale that flung the sea surface away in sheets of spume and were glad not to have to deal with it.

Twenty-four hours after *Explorer* picked us up, it dropped us at Port Lockroy to await the arrival of the *Tooluka*. A Kiwi yacht *Evohe* lay at anchor, and skipper Steve Kafka offered us berths until the *Tooluka* arrived. The mystery of the *Tooluka*'s location continued until two days later when Roger finally made contact. He had been delayed by storms in the Drake and a rescue of the Australian mountaineers who had been avalanched into a crevasse on the Peninsula. We worked with the film crew as we sailed our way back north up the Peninsula. I was fascinated anew by the coastline we had kayaked along. Had we reconnoitred it, we agreed, we would probably have forgone the attempt. The impression was one of too few landings too exposed to the weather.

It had been a rare privilege to witness and explore a world as beautiful as Antarctica on our own terms. We had travelled under our own steam, by simple means, unsupported for the most part, self-sufficient. We had many great memories.

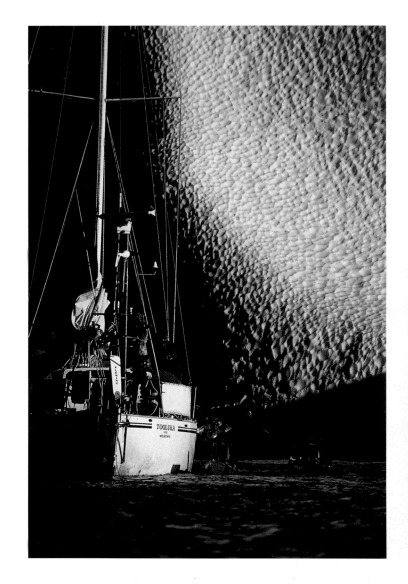

Alongside the *Tooluka*.

The southern parts of the Peninsula are huge and dramatic.

Antarctica to Ushuaia

Mark Jones

If uncertainty is the essence of adventure then this story could not be complete without relating the hapless trip back to Ushuaia from Antarctica on board the 14-metre sloop *Tooluka*. Uncertainty reigned like a bad genie – a genie intent on mischief conceived in scheming confinement.

Our journey back from the Peninsula was part of a documentary film deal. In return for the passage to Ushuaia, we had committed to five days of filming in addition to the footage we had already shot. Onboard the *Tooluka* was a film crew of three people, their cook and Roger Wallis, the skipper. Roger was about as nice a bloke as you could meet – welcoming, accommodating and generous of spirit. I felt comfortable in the silences between our conversations that, little by little, revealed a sailor of enormous experience and accomplishment. Roger possessed a pioneer spirit and operated with an assurance earned from long years at sea. His was the smallest craft that ran charter trips in Antarctic waters.

The weather fax confirmed our first delay, as an army of prickly fronts marched across the page, with bundles of isobars flexed for a fight. The *Tooluka* lay low for a couple of days inside Deception Island's flooded crater harbour. Batteries of rusting blubber oil tanks, rusting metal and dilapidated buildings from an old whaling station formed a bleak foreground to the desolate backdrop of Deception's scoria flanks.

Following the five days of filming we had nine days to reach Ushuaia to catch our 8 March flight home to New Zealand. It seemed more than enough time, but it never pays to count your penguin chicks south of the 55th parallel. A storm was raging in the Drake Passage. Outside the wind whined in the rigging, a mournful animal sound. It was 1 March, and our flight was the last available for a month. We should have listened to Roger and waited, but too soon we were bashing our way into the wind, careering and shuddering from crest to trough, hurtling through the black night. I was tethered to a stanchion and slowly freezing my way through my watch. Two hours of driving sleet and helming at an open wheel with hands half frozen, then below to bed down on a squab, pounded to queasy unconsciousness. During that wild, black night with three reefs in the main, a reckless tack tore the sail from luff to leech. A harrowing

We anchored near an old whaling station on Deception Island while waiting for a storm to pass in the Drake Passage.

sail change took place at midnight as the *Tooluka* lolled about with all the nautical aplomb of an iceberg. Then we were back to battling into the weather again, this time under a tiny but effective tri-sail.

One of the quirks of *Tooluka* was that its toilet flushed with water from its drinking water tanks. The tanks were low. We had hoped to top them up at Cuverville Island on the Peninsula, a sure bet earlier in the season. But icicles hung where days before water had trickled. Water was scarce on Deception Island, but during rain we found a trickle of surface water, and this was ladled into a plastic tank to act as a reserve if we ran out. Despite this measure, with eight people on board it was apparent that the water wasn't going to last the distance so the toilet was duly declared out of bounds.

We motor-sailed 50° off course, trying to reach some of the southwesterly air behind the low. My watch was 11pm to 1am. Staring ahead into the black night under starlight, I kept Sirius off the port side of the foresail. The galactic wake of the Milky Way stretched temporarily overhead, then a black curtain of cloud was drawn across the sky and nothing was visible except the mast, lit by the deck lights, stabbing wildly at the night. My whole world was reduced to the floating red dial of the compass, lurching about drunkenly in its globe of spirit. All else was darkness and the heaving sea. It was snowing, and the last half-hour was a struggle against the cold, with hands numb or throbbing and feet dead. Days dragged by, one blurred into the another, watches came and went, but somehow beneath the decks there was good cheer, good food and humour.

There was a bond between the three of us – a camaraderie, a pleasure, almost, in shared discomfort. Perhaps that is what defines adventurers: they suffer well. And suffer we three did, in the forward hold, with ceaseless dripping condensation and pounding that left us airborne at times.

Morning brought the news that the *Tooluka*'s water tanks were dry. Two more days of riding seas that seemed set to engulf the sloop at times, then the wind mysteriously died. We motor-sailed for half a day, then, in sight of Cape Horn, the motor clattered and died. What wind there was, was a northerly head wind. The water shortage was suddenly exacerbated. The humour in the situation was inescapable. My diary entry summed it up: 'Water situation means toilet is no longer a go. One has to squat on the bow, leaning out over the southern ocean on the bow rail facing aft. In the bigger swells one gets what is known as the "bidet effect", which may be mandatory soon as we are down to our last roll of toilet paper. All in all, things could be better.'

Roger mended the torn mainsail so we could make the best of what wind there was, and we lolled about, becalmed in sight of the Horn, notorious for its incessant wind and wild stormy weather.

I woke for my watch at 3am and found the *Tooluka* making slow but steady progress. Hills were discernible on either side of us, silhouetted against the stars. The radar had broken down sometime during the night, and the lights were off to conserve the batteries. We crept ahead past semi-submerged rocks and kept an eye on a stream of fishing boats chugging out toward the Horn. It was a golden dawn. I took it as a sign that our troubles were over,

Winter was starting to draw a chilly curtain over our Antarctic summer. It was time to leave.

Jonesy wrestles with the helm as the Drake Passage shows a different face on our return crossing.

but as the day progressed the head wind strengthened and an outgoing tide further retarded our progress.

The three of us were below mulling over the misfortunes of the yacht trip. The water, the storm, the becalming, the motor blowing up, radar going down, the toilet: it was a journey plagued by misfortune in an almost orchestrated series of events, the work of conspiratorial forces beyond our fathoming, intent on preventing us making that homeward flight.

Suddenly the sails were flapping and we heard Roger say in near-disbelief, 'Oh hell, we're going to go aground.' One of the film crew had let a sheet go too early, and we watched helplessly as the *Tooluka* shuddered to a halt and its keel hit the sand. 'Bugger,' said Roger.

Puerto Williams was only a short distance away, and the Chilean navy responded immediately to our distress call, informing us that because we had run aground on Argentinian soil they could not help us.

But assistance arrived a short while later in the form of an Argentinian fishing boat. Soon we were winching the sails up and once again beating windward. We turned down the Chilean navy's magnanimous offer of assistance once we tacked back into Chilean waters.

We berthed at Puerto Williams by dark, only to learn that the authorities would not allow us to depart because we had a disabled motor. We began to pack our kayaks. Ushuaia was only 50 kilometres away – a solid day's paddle would do it. Just when it seemed we would be saying goodbye to Roger and the *Tooluka* prematurely, they reconsidered and allowed the boat to travel in the hours of daylight. We decided to wait.

By morning the wind had deserted us once again so we towed *Tooluka* out into the middle of the channel with the inflatable, where it sat, drifting back toward the Cape on the tide, sails hanging lamely, not even raising a flap. We couldn't wait forever for the wind. A slim chance remained that we could reach Ushuaia by kayak. Perhaps the genie grew bored, perhaps he saw our packed kayaks and knew he was beaten, for as we floated forlornly, a passing yacht under motor offered us a tow. We made that flight with only hours to spare.

Postcript

Mark Jones

When we returned to New Zealand we were sometimes asked, 'Why did you do it?' It was difficult to answer because I felt those who needed to ask the question wouldn't fully understand my reasons. Society seems intent on conditioning us to lives of conservatism and security, on presenting risk as an unhealthy concept. And yet there is nothing more damaging to the human spirit than a life wrapped in cotton batting, a life of contrived safety and conformity.

The human soul knows no greater joy than watching the sun set on a new horizon. And the human spirit burns brightest when we are up against the odds, when we are giving our best account of ourselves. If we are overcome by the imagined risk, we may miss the elusive chance to live fully. This was the philosophy we had embraced; one we shared with many others drawn to adventure.

Antarctica has always attracted adventurers, romantics and dreamers in equal measure, for it is a place of the imagination. It is a place of mystery, a corner of the Earth apart, untamed. In a world that seems grubby by comparison, it promises vastness, simplicity and unsullied grandeur. People from all walks of life are fascinated by it, though only a lucky few find the means to get there.

Our journey had begun years before, and as we worked to make our dream reality we got to know one another very well. We were good mates, but adventure is an unforgiving forge for testing friendships. Sometimes the bonds between people become crystalline and brittle; sometimes they become tempered with a hard, enduring quality. Respect is the ingredient that makes the difference. The three of us were closer then than we had ever been, and I felt the bonds would last forever. I still do.

It was a shared experience, but it was also an intensely personal one. I slayed my own dragons along that coast, put to rest my own frailties and arguments for my limitations. My horizons expanded to encompass a larger world and a greater sense of my own dimensions.

We had lived on the ragged edge of that land, between relentless ocean and implacable ice. But, like the twilight hour between darkness and day, it lacked the harshness of either and yet was somehow more than both – a zone of unforgettable beauty and dramatic change. To live out of a kayak, surrounded by nature at its most elemental, with nothing but your skill and love for what you are doing, is to experience life stripped bare. What remains is the essential core of living: friendship, endeavour and the beating heart of the wild.

Friendship, endeavour and the beating heart of the wild.

Equipment

Marcus Waters

One of the principal problems when preparing gear for our expedition was lack of information. Nobody had paddled in Antarctic waters for the distance or duration that we were contemplating. Mostly we took educated guesses. Our practice trips in Fiordland and in the terminal lake of the Tasman Glacier were invaluable as we were able to test our Macpac paddling suits and brainstorm other aspects of our equipment.

Polar Bear Kayaks

Ron Augustin from Paddling Perfection in Auckland, New Zealand, designed a kayak that would suit the rigours of polar travel: strong, stable and relatively quick. He devised the Polar Bear Sea Kayak by making major structural refinements to his tried and proven Sea Bear kayak design. In order to accommodate both speed and the storage capacity we needed, Ron lengthened the Sea Bear by 400 millimetres to produce a relatively quick yet stable kayak. The Polar Bear ended up 5,900 millimetres long and 620 millimetres across the beam. It was constructed from the strongest material commercially available – a two-layer laminated kevlar hull with a three-layer reinforced bow (for bashing into brash ice). The kayak had a fibreglass deck, three storage hatches (320-litre total storage capacity) and sealed compartments. The cockpit was lined with closed-cell foam for warmth. Load-bearing handles were added forward and aft of the cockpit for carrying. All the components were tested in the deep freeze for resistance to freezing temperatures. The reinforced rudder system, 25 per cent stronger than standard, was a great idea. Weighing around 35 kilograms unloaded and 90 kilograms fully loaded, the kayaks were excellent and handled abuse amazingly well, even the pounding they got on the deck of the *Tooluka* sailing back to Ushuaia.

Polar Bear Sea Kayak by Paddling Perfection, Auckland, New Zealand

- length 5,900 millimetres
- beam 620 millimetres
- storage capacity: 320 litres, three hatches
- weight 35 kilograms unloaded

- material: hull: two-layer kevlar, with reinforced bow (three-layer kevlar); deck: fibreglass; cockpit insulation: closed-cell foam
- reinforced rudder system

Paddles

The paddle is the sea kayaker's engine: no paddle, no propulsion. We used Prijon kevlar-carbon sea kayak paddles, supplied by Donald Calder of Sunspots, Rotorua, New Zealand. Our main concern was strength and these paddles performed well. Before the expedition, Graham and Jonesy turned theirs into split paddles for easy stowage. In spite of my concern and refusal to do the same, this did not reduce the strength of the paddles. (On the way back to Ushuaia, Graham and Jonesy insisted that I saw my paddle in half. Amid howls of mirth, and in spite of my usual fastidious measure-thrice-cut-once approach, I ended up with two odd lengths.) All three of us carried a spare paddle under the rear bungies in case we broke or lost a paddle.

Clothing

There was debate over a one-piece drysuit versus the convenience of a two-piece paddling suit. In the end, we trusted our ability to Eskimo roll the kayaks, avoiding the dreaded swim, and went for the breathability of XCR GORE-TEX paddling trousers and jacket. The material was the latest GORE-TEX offering from Gore and promised 30 per cent more breathability. The collars were simple velcro seals, great for ventilation, with rubber-sealed wrist cuffs. The trousers were one piece, with built-in feet. Macpac based the design on the waterproof trousers they make for air force pilots. After the Fiordland trip it became obvious that the GORE-TEX feet were going to wear out quickly, so Macpac reinforced the feet and seat areas. Despite becoming totally salt-encrusted, the garments worked very well.

Over the jackets we wore XCR GORE-TEX life vests. These were based on the Macpac whitewater life jackets but contained less foam to reduce their bulk and make them easier for forward paddling. They had the usual Macpac features of side adjustments, front pockets and towlines.

Under the outer garments we wore the Macpac underall, a sleeveless bodysuit made of Polartec 200-weight fleece. It proved fantastic, hugging the body for ease of movement, and always warm. Depending on the day, a thin Macpac polyprop or Merino wool top and another 200-weight pullover jersey could be added. When paddling, perspiration was often a problem, but the jackets allowed for ventilation and the fleece garments stayed warm despite being damp a lot of the time.

For headgear there was the option of a Macpac Neotherm numbskull cap, a fleece hat or a sun hat, depending on the temperature. On misty, snowy days it was usually enough to pull up the hood on the paddling jacket. During most of February it was warm enough for the peaked sun hat.

Footwear was a tricky issue. We needed something warm that could also get wet as we landed or launched the kayaks. Gill kevlar/GORE-TEX sailing boots fitted the bill. These had a sturdy rubber sole with leather around the foot. The calf-length boots, which kept our feet dry during most landings, were made of a tough kevlar material. Inevitably they became damp with constant use (in fact Graham and I developed painful chilblains) but otherwise worked well. I wore mine for more than 40 consecutive days (which meant keeping your distance when I took them off).

Hands were another problem. If they were dripping seawater and were then exposed to the cold Antarctic air, they would have become frozen lumps in just one or two minutes. Nylon pogies weren't suitable. Veteran New Zealand adventure racer Steve Gurney came to the rescue with his closed-cell foam pogies. These were warm five-millimetre foam gloves that held their moulded hand shape and were easy to get on and off. With a tail wind, our hands became very cold as polar air was forced into the pogies. For these occasions we carried Neotherm mitts, with a clever slit across the palm so that we could use our fingers if necessary. The team all returned home with 10 fingers each. Thanks, Steve!

At the end of every day we wriggled out of wet paddling gear and into Macpac down jackets filled with 180 grams of goose down. We lived in these when off the water. The jackets packed down into a small bundle and stayed dry in our dry bags.

Paddling clothing

- polypro top, other 200-weight fleece
- 200-weight underalls
- GORE-TEX paddle jacket
- underpants
- GORE-TEX paddle pants

- socks
- hooties (Macpac fleece booties)
- kayak boots
- numbskull hat, sunhat
- closed-cell foam pogies

- Neotherm mitts
- ski goggles (unused)
- sunglasses
- neoprene face guard (unused)

Land clothing

- polypro top
- 200-weight fleece
- down jacket
- polypro pants
- underpants

- fleece pants
- sock
- gloves, thin
- gloves, thick with outer
- fleece hat

- neck muff (unused)
- boots
- pac towel

Personal gear

Most of our personal gear we carried in dry bags (tough, waterproof bags with a sealable top). Each paddler carried an array of dry bags to transport clothing and sleeping bags. Although the kayak compartments were relatively dry, water would eventually find its way into them.

- dry bags
- sleeping bag, stuff sack
- sleeping bag liner
- Therma rest

- closed-cell foam mat
- book (one each)
- diary
- toothbrush and paste

- personal creams
- lip balm
- sunblock

Tent

The team used the Macpac expedition Spectrum. Given that there were no major arguments over the 36 days, it must have been large enough! Double poles and valances strengthened with sail repair cloth made sure the tent withstood the katabatic winds. The double vestibules were big enough for cooking and storing gear. We always loaded rocks and snow onto the valances and extended the guy ropes – you never could be sure when the wind was going to hit!

Stoves

Supplied by MSR, these were their Expedition XPG stoves, fuelled with white spirits. Plenty of fuel (0.8 litres per day) was needed to melt ice for water.

Bags

Colour-coded nylon bags enabled easy location of gear – usually the stove, billies and cups, or the drink and food – and saved fumbling around in the boats or having to ask everyone, twice, where the cups were.

Party equipment

- shovel
- tent brush
- two MSR Expedition XPG stoves
- stove repair kit
- fuel bottles and fuel (30 litres)
- lighter, matches
- pots and billies (a big aluminium pot was excellent: the thinner stainless steel billy burned food, no matter how much it was stirred)
- cup, bowl, spoon
- Leatherman pocket knife
- repair kit (assortment of thread, needles, bits and pieces)
- spare string
- colour-coded nylon bags
- toilet paper

Food

We needed food that was light, compact yet nutritious. We researched books on Antarctic expeditions and found very detailed food information on the Ice Trek website: www.icetrek.com. We needed to get the right combination of fat, protein and carbohydrate. Doing hard work in the cold Antarctic environment, it is more weight efficient (i.e. calories per gram) to get a greater proportion of energy from fat than from carbohydrates. We worked with a diet of 6,000 calories per day, but this was an overestimate: we took olive oil and anhydrous milk fat that we did not need. Before we left we shrink-wrapped each individual lunch pack, which was convenient and easy to handle. The thermoses we took allowed for hot drinks during the day. These were a godsend.

The menu ended up as follows:
Breakfast: Hubbard's porridge with protein powder added. Tea and coffee.
Lunch: vacuum-sealed ration packs of dried fruit, Propel bar, Vitazone bar, Moro bar, sweets, cheese, crackers, salami.
Dinner: soup followed by BackCountry Foods five-person freeze-dried meal with additional fat added before drying.
Plus 2 Vitazone bars each with tea.

Navigation

We used British and American maps of the Antarctic Peninsula that we ordered through Trans Pacific Marine in Auckland. We photocopied the relevant sections and divided the trip into 16 A3 maps which we laminated. Jonesy scoured books, articles and research papers, and added jottings and points of interest to the maps.

We carried a hand-held Garmin GPS, but used it very little. We were originally concerned that sea ice might make map reading difficult, but by all accounts our season was relatively ice-free and navigation was not a problem. On the misty days we followed bearings on our standard magnetic deck compasses.

Communication

Tait Communications New Zealand provided two Orca Elan hand-held VHF radios and enough batteries to last for the five weeks of the expedition. These allowed line of sight communication (about 30 kilometres) and were used to contact the pick-up vessel when it was within range. The radios were also very useful when we were completing our final preparations in Ushuaia, allowing us to keep in contact with each other and consult on purchase decisions. We also had an HF radio with crystals added for the appropriate frequencies. Although the HF could transmit over long distances it was subject to the vagaries of atmospheric conditions, and communication was impossible a good portion of the time. We also carried an emergency locator beacon.

Technical gear

We carried a range of technical hardware. Most of the technical hardware (i.e. ice screws, pulleys, jumar, grappling hook, crampons, etc) we took in anticipation of dragging and manhandling the kayaks over sea ice. In the end, the gear was redundant, but another sea kayak party could encounter more sea ice and the equipment would be vital. The rope and slings were useful for securing the boats each night to avoid their being blown away in strong winds.

- hand pump
- flares
- grappling hook for paddle
- eight carabiners
- 25-metre 8.8 rope
- two slings

- two pulleys
- two ice axes
- one hammer
- three sets instep crampons
- two prusiks
- binoculars

- lightweight jumar
- two rock pitons

Repair kit

- two rolls duct tape
- 8- and 12-gauge wire
- electrical wire
- needle-nose vice-grips
- hacksaw blade

- hand-awl and thread
- one length of Selleys 'Need It' mouldable repair compound
- sail sticky-cloth
- nylon braid

- fibreglass cloth and resin
- tube of Ados f2 contact adhesive
- tube of neoprene glue

Video and still camera equipment

It would have made great sense to have used one camera brand so that lenses could be swapped between cameras. Unfortunately, Graham shoots with a Nikon and Jonesy with a Canon so we carried separate sets of still equipment. A major goal of the expedition was to shoot a documentary for American Adventure Productions. This was shot with JVC digital video cameras. In order to mount the video cameras on our boats, Jonesy added a bracket onto the front hatch of two of the kayaks. This bracket could hold an ice axe in a horizontal position. A clamp could then be attached to the ice axe to support the video camera. We were keen to get a system that could accommodate a variety of camera angles (as this makes for happy editors and interesting viewing). The system worked well, with the one drawback that the kayaker couldn't operate the video camera from the cockpit of the kayak; someone else had to come alongside, line the camera up and turn it on.

Stills gear

- one Canon EOS 50
- one Nikon F9
- two 17–35-millimetre lenses
- two 28–80-millimetre lenses
- two 80–300-millimetre lenses
- assorted filters
- two flash units
- three batteries for each
- one light tripod
- 100 rolls of Kodak slide film
- two Pelican waterproof cases
- one Leica compact

Video gear

- two PD100 DVC and one waterproof housing
- one PC10 DVC and waterproof housing
- 40 one-hour tapes
- logbooks
- sufficient batteries for 100 hours operation
- remote control unit and cable
- mounting bracket and clamp to attach unit to ice axe/boat
- two microphones
- extension pole for variations in camera angles
- one fluffy (microphone cover)
- waterproof Pelican case

Wish we'd left behind

Additional fat (olive oil and anhydrous milk fat). In the end we didn't need the extra calories that we budgeted for.

Disputed item

The tent brush (Graham and Marcus for, Jonesy against).

Wish we'd taken

A chess set.

Best innovation

Closed-cell foam pogies.